Frederic William Henry Myers

The Renewal of Youth, and Other Poems

Frederic William Henry Myers

The Renewal of Youth, and Other Poems

ISBN/EAN: 9783337006334

Printed in Europe, USA, Canada, Australia, Japan

Cover: Foto ©Thomas Meinert / pixelio.de

More available books at **www.hansebooks.com**

THE

RENEWAL OF YOUTH

AND OTHER POEMS.

BY

FREDERIC W. H. MYERS.

London:
MACMILLAN AND CO.
1882

Cambridge:
PRINTED BY C. J. CLAY, M.A. & SON,
AT THE UNIVERSITY PRESS.

DEDICATED TO MY WIFE.

M.

∗ This volume contains (1) *The Renewal of Youth* and other poems as yet unpublished : (2) various pieces already printed in the *Fortnightly Review* and *Macmillan's Magazine*, and (3) some pieces published in a small volume of *Poems* which appeared in 1870, and which has long been out of print. Less than half of that volume, however, is incorporated into the present one. *S. Paul* is now published in a separate form, and many shorter pieces have been omitted here.

JULY, 1882.

CONTENTS.

PART I.

	PAGE
THE TRANSLATION OF FAITH	1
S. JOHN THE BAPTIST	10
AMMERGAU	29
THE IMPLICIT PROMISE OF IMMORTALITY	46
ON ART AS AN AIM IN LIFE	58
TWO SISTERS	72
SIMMENTHAL	76
ON AN INVALID	79
WOULD GOD IT WERE EVENING	82
WOULD GOD IT WERE MORNING	83
HIGH TIDE AT MIDNIGHT	84
ON A GRAVE AT GRINDELWALD	85
AFTER AN INTERVIEW	86
LOVE AND FAITH	88

	PAGE
A Prayer	91
A Last Appeal	92
Teneriffe	93
A Letter from Newport	98
Epithalamium	102
Stanzas on Shelley	105
In Henry VII.'s Chapel, Westminster Abbey	109
Stanzas on Mr Watts' collected Works.	112

PART II.

The Passing of Youth	121
Sweet Seventeen	140
Ah, no more Questions, no more Fears	142
Who to the Grave Child-Eyes could teach	143
Arethusa	145
Auf Flügeln des Gesanges	147
Unsatisfactory	149
Satisfactory	151
Oh never kiss me; stand apart	155
Hesione	156
Nora	160
Though Words of Ice be spoken	163

CONTENTS.

	PAGE
PHYLLIS	164
WHEN SUMMER EVEN SOFTLY DIES	166
A CRY FROM THE STALLS	169
THE BALLERINA'S PROGRESS, OR THE POETRY OF MOTION	172
I SAW, I SAW THE LOVELY CHILD	176
CYDIPPE	178
LOVER'S SONG	180
ANTE DIEM	182
WHY SHOULD I STRIVE TO EXPRESS IT?	185
PREEXISTENCE	186
A SONG	187
HONOUR	189
ELODIA	192
GABRIELLE	194
ÉCHOS DU TEMPS PASSÉ	196
THE RENEWAL OF YOUTH	199

PART I.

THE TRANSLATION OF FAITH.*

I.

HIGH in the midst the pictured Pentecost
Showed in a sign the coming of the Ghost,
And round about were councils blazoned
Called by the Fathers in a day long dead,
Who once therein, as well the limner paints,
Upbuilt the faith delivered to the saints.

Without the council-hall, in dawning day,
The mass of men had left a narrow way

* Public Session of the Œcumenical Council, in St. Peter's, Rome, January 6, Feast of the Epiphany, 1870.

Where ever-burning lamps enlock the tomb
In golden glamour and in golden gloom.
There on the earth is peace, and in the air
An aspiration of eternal prayer;
So many a man in immemorial years
Has scarcely seen that image for his tears,
So oft have women found themselves alone
With Christ and Mary on the well-worn stone.

Thereby the conclave of the bishops went,
With grave brows cherishing a dim intent,
As men who travelled on their eve of death
From every shore that man inhabiteth,
Not knowing wherefore, for the former things
Fade from old eyes of bishops and of kings.

With crimson raiment one from Bozrah came,
On brow and breast the rubies flashed in flame;
And this from Tyre, from Tunis that, and he
From Austral islands and the Austral sea;—
And many a swarthy face and stern was there,

And many a man who knows deep things and rare,
Knows the Chaldaic and the Coptic rite,
The Melchian-Greek and Ebio-Maronite,
Strange words of men who speak from long ago,
Lived not our lives, but what we know not know.

And some there were who never shall disdain
The Orders of their poverty and pain;
Amidst all pomp preferring for their need
The simple cowl and customary weed,—
Some white and Carmelite, and some alway
In gentle habit of Franciscan grey.

And lo, the sovereign Pontiff, Holy Sire,
Fulfilled anew the Catholic desire;—
Beneath the scroll of Peter's charge unfurled
He sat him at the centre of the world,
Attending till the deeds of God began,
And the One Sacrifice was slain for man.

But yet to me was granted to behold

A greater glory than the Pontiff's gold;—
To my purged eyes before the altar lay
A figure dreamlike in the noon of day;
Nor changed the still face, nor the look thereon,
At ending of the endless antiphon,
Nor for the summoned saints and holy hymn
Grew to my sight less delicate and dim:—
How faint, how fair that immaterial wraith!
But, looking long, I saw that she was Faith.

II.

Last in the midst of all a patriarch came,
Whose nation none durst ask him, nor his name,
Yet 'mid the Eastern sires he seemed as one
Fire-nurtured at the springing of the sun,
And in robe's tint was likest-hued to them
Who wear the Babylonian diadem.
His brows black yet and white unfallen hair
Set in strange frame the face of his despair,
And I despised not, nor can God despise,

The silent splendid anger of his eyes.
A hundred years of search for flying Truth
Had left them glowing with no gleam of youth,
A hundred years of vast and vain desire
Had lit and filled them with consuming fire;
Therethrough I saw his fierce eternal soul
Gaze from beneath that argent aureole;
I saw him bow his hoar majestic head,
I heard him, and he murmured, "Faith is dead."

Through arch and avenue the rumour ran,
Shed from the mighty presence of the man;
Through arch and avenue and vault and aisle
He cast the terror of his glance awhile,
Then rose at once and spake with hurrying breath,
As one who races with a racing Death.

"How long ago our fathers followed far
That false flame of the visionary star!
Oh better, better had it been for them
To have perished on the edge of Bethlehem,

Or ere they saw the comet stoop and stay,
And knew the shepherds, and became as they!
Better for us to have been, as men may be,
Sages and silent by the Eastern sea,
Than thus in new delusion to have brought
Myrrh of our prayer, frankincense of our thought,
For One whom knowing not we held so dear,
For One who sware it, but who is not here.
Better for you, this shrine when ye began,
An earthquake should have hidden it from man,
Than thus through centuries of pomp and pain
To have founded and have finished it in vain,—
To have vainly arched the labyrinthine shade,
And vainly vaulted it, and vainly made
For saints and kings an everlasting home
High in the dizzying glories of the dome.
Since not one minute over hall or Host
Flutters the peerless presence of the Ghost,
Nor falls at all, for art or man's device,
On mumbled charm and mumming sacrifice,—

But either cares not, or forspent with care
Has flown into the infinite of air.

Apollo left you when the Christ was born,
Jehovah when the temple's veil was torn,
And now, even now, this last time and again,
The presence of a God has gone from men.
Live in your dreams, if ye must live, but I
Will find the light, and in the light will die."

III.

At that strange speech the sons of men amazed
Each on the other tremulously gazed,
When lo, herself,—herself the age to close,—
From where she lay the very Faith arose;
She stood as never she shall stand again,
And for an instant manifest to men:—
In figure like the Mother-maid who sees
The deepest heart of hidden mysteries,
On that strange night when from her eyes she shed

A holy glory on the painter's bed,
And Agnes and the angels hushed awhile,
Won by her sadness sweeter than a smile.
Such form she wore, nor yet henceforth will care
That form, or form at all, on earth to wear;
For those sweet eyes, which once, with flag unfurled,
So many a prince would follow through the world,--
That face, the light of dreams, the crown of day,
Lo, while we looked on her, was rapt away;
O mystic end and o evanished queen!
When shall we see thee as our sires have seen?

And yet, translated from the Pontiff's side,
She did not die, o say not that she died!
She died not, died not, o the faint and fair!
She could not die, but melted into air.

In that high dome I neither know nor say
What Power and Presence was alive that day,
No, nor what Faith, in what transfigured form,
Rode on the ghostly spaces of the storm:

For sight of eyes nor ear with hearing knew
That windless wind that where it listed blew;
Yet seeing eyes and ears that hear shall be
As dust and nothingness henceforth for me,
Who once have felt the blowing Spirit roll
Life on my life, and on my soul a Soul.

And first the conclave and the choir, and then
The immeasurable multitude of men,
Bowed and fell down, bowed and fell down, as though
A rushing mighty wind had laid them low;
Yea to all hearts a revelation came,
As flying thunder and as flying flame;
A moment then the vault above him seemed
To each man as the heaven that he had dreamed;
A moment then the floor whereon he trod
Became the pavement of the courts of God;
And in the aisles was silence, in the dome
Silence, and no man knew that it was Rome.

ROME, *Jan.* 7, 1870.

SAINT JOHN THE BAPTIST.

O Jesus, if one minute, if one hour
Thou wouldst come hitherward and speak with
    John!
Nay, but be present only, nay, but come:
And I shall look, and as I look on thee
Find in thine eyes the answer and the end.

And I am he who once in Nazareth,
A child, nor knowing yet the prophet's woe,
In childly fashion sought thee, and even then
Perceived a mute withdrawal, open eyes
That drooped not for caressing, brows that knew
Dominion, and the babe already king.

Ah Mary, but thou also, thou as I,
With eager tremulous humilities,
With dumb appeal and tears that dared not flow,
Hast laid thy loving arms about the boy,
And clasped him wistfully and felt him far.

And ever as I grew his loveliness
Grew with me, and the yearning turned to pain.
Then said I,—"Nay, my friends, no need is now
For John to tarry with you; I have seen,
I have known him; I go hence, and all alone
I carry Jesus with me till I die."

And that same day, being past the Passover,
I gat me to the desert, and stayed to see
Joseph and Mary holding each a hand
Of one that followed meekly; and I was gone,
And with strange beasts in the great wilderness
I laid me, fearing nothing, and hardly knew
On what rough meat in what unwonted ways
I throve, or how endured the frost and fire;

But moaned and carried in my heart for him
A first and holy passion, boy for boy,
And loved the hills that look on Nazareth
And every fount that pours upon the plain.

Then once with trembling knees and heart afire
I ran, I sought him: but my Lord at home
Bright in the full face of the dawning day
Stood at his carpentry, and azure air
Inarched him, scattered with the glittering green:
I saw him standing, I saw his face, I saw
His even eyebrows over eyes grey-blue,
From whence with smiling there looked out on me
A welcome and a wonder,—"Mine so soon?"—
Ah me, how sweet and unendurable
Was that confronting beauty of the boy!
Jesus, thou knowest I had no answer then,
But leapt without a word, and flung away,
And dared not think thereof, and looked no more.

And after that with wonder rose in me

Strange speech of early prophets, and a tale
First learnt and last forgotten, song that fell
With worship from the lonely Israelites,
Simeon and Anna; for these twain as one
Fast by the altar and in the courts of God
Led a long age in fair expectancy.
For all about them swept the heedless folk,
Unholy folk and market merchandise,
They each from each took courage, and with prayer
Made ready for the coming of a King.
So, when the waves of Noe on forest and hill
Ran ruinous, and all herbs had lost the life
Of greenness and the memory of air,
The cedar-trees alone on Lebanon
Spread steadfastly invulnerable arms.

That was no sleep when clear the vision came,
Bright in the night and truer than the day:—
For there with brows newborn and locks that flew
Was Adam, and his eyes remembered God ;
And Eve, already fallen, already in woe,

Knowing a sweeter promise for the pain;
And after these, unknown, unknowable,
The grave gigantic visage of dead men,
With looks that are not ours, with speech to say
That no man dares interpret; then I saw
A maiden such as countrymen afield
Greet reverently, and love her as they see;
And after that a boy with face so fair,
With such a glory and a wonder in it,
I grieved to find him born upon the earth
To man's life and the heritage of sin;
And last of all that Mary whom I knew
Stood with such parted lips and face aglow
As long-since when the angel came to her;
And all these pointed forward, and I knew
That each was prophet and singer and sire and seer,
That each was priest and mother and maid and king,
With longing for the babe of Nazareth,
For that man-child who should be born and reign.

And once again I saw him, in latter days
Fraught with a deeper meaning, for he came
To my baptizing, and the infinite air
Blushed on his coming, and all the earth was still;
Gently he spake; I answered; God from heaven
Called, and I hardly heard him, such a love
Streamed in that orison from man to man.
Then shining from his shoulders either-way
Fell the flood Jordan, and his kingly eyes
Looked in the east, and star-like met the sun.
Once in no manner of similitude,
And twice in thunderings and thrice in flame,
The Highest ere now hath shown him secretly;
But when from heaven the visible Spirit in air
Came verily, lighted on him, was alone,
Then knew I, then I said it, then I saw
God in the voice and glory of a man.

And one will say, "And wilt thou not forget
The unkindly king that hath forgotten thee?"
Nay, I remember; like my sires who sat

Faithful and stubborn by Euphrates' stream,
Nor in their age forgot Jerusalem,
Nor reared their children for another joy.

O Jesus, if thou knewest, if thou couldst know,
How in my heart through sleep and pain and prayer
Thy royalty remaineth; how thy name
Falls from my lips unbidden, and the dark
Is thick with lying shades that are not thou,—
Couldst thou imagine it, O tender soul!
At least in vision thou wouldst come to me;
I should not only hear of dumb that sing
And lame that leap around thee, and all thy ways
Joyful, and on thy breast another John.

How should I not remember? Is dusk of day
Forgetful, or the winter of the sun?
Have these another glory? or whom have I
In all the world but Jesus for my love?
Whereinsoever breath may rise and die
Their generations follow on, and earth

Each in their kind replenisheth anew,
Only like him she bears not nor hath borne
One in her endless multitude of men.

And these were ever about me; morn by morn
Mine eyes again desired him, and I saw
The thronging Hebrews thicken, and my heart
Sank, and the prophet served another day.

Yet sometimes when by chance the rulers came,
Encharnelled in their fatness, men that smile,
Sit in high seats, and swell with their desire,
My strong limbs shook, and my heart leapt and
    fell
With passion of sheer scorn, with speech that slew,
With glances that among them running dealt
Damnation, as on Egypt ran the flame.
For such men never when I look on them
Can keep their pride or smiling, but their brow
Droops from its base dominion, and their voice
Rings hollower with a stirring fear within,

Till flushes chill to paleness, and at length
From self-convicted eyes evanisheth
The false and fickle lumour of their joy.

For quick and fitfully with feast and song
Men make a tumult round them, and console
With sudden sport a momentary woe;
But if thou take one hence, and set him down
In some strange jeopardy on enormous hills,
Or swimming at night alone upon the sea,
His lesser life falls from him, and the dream
Is broken which had held him unaware,
And with a shudder he feels his naked soul
In the great black world face to face with God.

This also for that miserable man
Is a worse trouble than his heart can know,
That in the strait and sodden ways of sin
He has made him alien to the plenteous day,
Cut off from friendliness with woods that wave
And happy pasture and carousing sea,

And whatsoever loving things enjoy
Simply the kind simplicity of God.
For these are teachers; not in vain His seers
Have dwelt in solitudes and known that God
High up in open silence and thin air
More presently reveals him, having set
His chiefest temples on the mountain-tops,
His kindling altar in the hearts of men.
And these I knew with peace and lost with pain,
And oft for whistling wind and desert air
Lamented, and in dreams was my desire
For the flood Jordan, for the running sound
And broken glitters of the midnight moon.
But now all this fades from me, and the life
Of prophecy, and summers that I knew.
Yea, and though once I looked on many men
And spake them sweet and bitter speech, and heard
Such secrets as a tempest of the soul
Once in a lifetime washes black and bare
From desperate recesses of shut sin,
Yet all is quite forgotten, and to-day

From the strange past no sign remains with me
But simple and tremendous memories
Of morning and of even and of God.

Ah me, ah me, for if a man desire
Gold or great wealth or marriage with a maid,
How easily he wins her, having served
Seven years perchance, and counting that for gain;
But whoso wants God only and lets life go,
Seeks him with sorrow, and pursues him far,
And finds him weeping, and in no long time
Again the High and Unapproachable
Evanishing escapeth, and that man
Forgets the life and struggle of the soul,
Falls from his hope, and dreams it was a dream.

Yet back again perforce with sorrow and shame
Who once hath known him must return, nor long
Can cease from loving, nor endures alone
The dreadful interspace of dreams and day,
Once quick with God; nor is content as those

Who look into each other's eyes and seek
To find one strong enough to uphold the earth,
Or sweet enough to make it heaven: aha,
Whom seek they or whom find? for in all the world
There is none but thee, my God, there is none but thee.

And this it is that links together as one
The sad continual companies of men;
Not that the old earth stands, and Ararat
Endureth, and Euphrates till to-day
Remembers where God walked beside the stream;
Nay rather that souls weary and hearts afire
Have everywhere besought him, everywhere
Have found and found him not; and age to age,
Though all else pass and fail, delivereth
At least the great tradition of their God.

For even thus on Ur and Mahanaim
By Asian rivers gathering to the sea,

When the huge stars shone gold, and dim and still
Dewed in the dusk the innocent yearlings lay,
With constant eyes the serious shepherd-men
Renewed the old desiring, sought again
The mute eternal Presence; and for these
Albeit sometimes the sundering firmament
One moment to no bodily sense revealed
Unspeakably an imminence of love;—
Yet by no song have our forefathers known
To set the invisible in sight of men,
Nor in all years have any wisdom found
But patient hope and dumb humility.

  Yea, Lord, I know it, teach me yet 'anew
With what a fierce and patient purity
I must confront the horror of the world.
For very little space on either hand
Parts the sane mind from madness; very soon
By the intenser pressure of one thought
Or clearer vision of one agony
The soothfast reason trembles, all things fade

In blackness, and the demon enters in.—
I would I never may be left of thee,
O God, my God, in whatsoever ill;
Be present while thou strikest, thus shall grow
At least a solemn patience with the pain;—
When thou art gone, what is there in the world
Seems not dishonoured, desperate with sin?
The stars are threatful eyeballs, and the air
Hangs thick and heavy with the wrath of God,
And even pure pity in my heart congeals
To idle anger with thy ways and thee,
Nor any care for life remains to me,
Nor trust in love, nor fellowship with men,
But past my will the exasperated brain
Thinks bitter thoughts, and I no more am John.

It is not when man's heart is nighest heaven
He hath most need of servant-seraphim,—
Albeit that height be holy and God be still,
And lifted up he dies with his desire,
That only once the Highest for dear love's sake

Would set himself in whispers of a man :—
Nay, but much rather when one flat on earth
Knows not which way to grovel, or where to flee
From the overmastering agony of sin,
Then his deed tears him till he find one pure
To know it and forgive: "For God," saith he,
" Still on the unjust sends unchangeable
These scornful boons of summer and of rain,
And howsoever I fall, with dawn and day
Floods me, and splendidly ignores my sin."

And how should pity and anger cease, or shame
Have done with blushes, till the prophet know
That God not yet hath quite despaired of men?
Oh that the heavens were rent and one came down
Who saw men's hurt with kindlier eyes than mine,
Fiercelier than I resented every wrong,
Sweated more painful drops than these that flow
In nightly passion for my people's sin,—
Died with it, lived beyond it,—nay, what now?
If this indeed were Jesus, this the Lamb

Whom age by age the temple-sacrifice
Not vainly had prefigured, and if so
In one complete and sacred agony
He lifted all the weight of all the world,—
And if men knew it, and if men clung to him
With desperate love and present memory,—
I know not how,—till all things fail in fire;
That were enough, and, o my God, for them,
For them there might be peace, but not for me.

And even Elias often on the hills
Towered in a flaming sunset, sick at heart;
Often with bare breast on the dewy earth
Lay all night long, and all night comfortless
Poured his abounding bitterness of soul:
I know that not without a wail he bore
The solitude of prophets till that day
When death divine and unbelievable
Blazed in the radiant chariot and blown fire,
Whereof the very memory melts mine eyes
And holds my heart with wonder : can it be

That thus obscurely to his ministers
Jehovah portioneth eternal love?

Here in the hazardous joy of woman and man
Consider with how sad and eager eyes
They lean together, and part, and gaze again,
Regretting that they cannot in so brief time,
With all that sweet abandonment, outpour
Their flowing infinity of tenderness.
God's fashion is another; day by day
And year by year he tarrieth; little need
The Lord should hasten; whom he loves the most
He seeks not oftenest, nor wooes him long,
But by denial quickens his desire,
And in forgetting best remembers him,
Till that man's heart grows humble and reaches out
To the least glimmer of the feet of God,
Grass on the mountain-tops, or the early note
Of wild birds in the hush before the day,—
Wherever sweetly in the ends of the earth
Are fragments of a peace that knows not man.

Then on our utter weakness and the hush
Of hearts exhausted that can ache no more,
On such abeyance of self and swoon of soul
The Spirit hath lighted oft, and let men see
That all our vileness alters God no more
Than our dimmed eyes can quench the stars in
    heaven :—
From years ere years were told, through all the sins,
Unknown sins of innumerable men,
God is himself for ever, and shows to-day
As erst in Eden, the eternal hope.

Wherefore if anywise from morn to morn
I can endure a weary faithfulness,
From minute unto minute calling low
On God who once would answer, it may be
He hath a waking for me, and some surprise
Shall from this prison set the captive free
And love from fears and from the flesh the soul.

For even thus beside Gennesaret

In solemn night some demon-haunted man
Runs from himself, and nothing knows in heaven
But blackness, yet around him unaware
With standing hills and high expectancy,
With early airs and shuddering and calm,
The enormous morning quickens, and lake and tree
Perceive each other dimly in a dream:
And when at last with bodily frame forspent
He throws him on the beach to sleep or die,
That very moment rises full and fair
Thy sun, o Lord, the sun that brings the day.

I wait it; I have spoken; even now
This hour may set me in one place with God.
I hear a wantoning in Herod's hall,
And feet that seek me; very oft some chance
Leaps from the folly and the wine of kings;—
O Jesus, spirit and spirit, soul and soul,—
O Jesus, I shall seek thee, I shall find,
My love, my master, find thee, though I be
Least, as I know, of all men woman-born.

AMMERGAU.*

1.

"WHERE is he gone? O men and maidens, where
Is gone the fairest amid all the fair?
Mine eyes desire him, and with dawning day
My heart goes forth to find him on the way."

Ah, how that music lingers, and again
Returns the dying sweetness of the strain!
How clearly on my inner sense is borne
The fair fresh beauty of the mountain morn,
And cries of flocks afar, and mixed with these
The green delightful tumult of the trees,—

* Celebration of the Passion-Play at Ober-Ammergau, in Bavaria, June 25, 1870.

The birds that o'er us from the upper day
Threw flitting shade, and went their airy way,—
The bright-robed chorus and the silent throng,
And that first burst and sanctity of song!

In such a place with eager faces fair
Sat men of old in bright Athenian air,
Heard in such wise the folk of Theseus sing
Their welcome to the world-forsaken king,—
Awaited thus between the murmuring trees
The whisper of appeased Eumenides,
Till breath came thick and eyes no more could see
For sweet prevision of the end to be.

But ah, how hard a task to set again
The living Christ among the homes of men!
Have we not grown too faithless or too wise
For this old tale of many mysteries?
Will not this passion of the peasants seem
Like children's tears for terror of a dream?—

AMMERGAU.

"Hosanna! whoso in the Highest Name,
Hosanna! cometh as Elias came,
Him Israel hails and honours, Israel showers
Before him all her hopes and all her flowers."—

O Son of God! O blessed vision, stay!
O be my whole life centred in to-day!
Ah, let me dream that this indeed is He,
Mine eyes desired Him, and at last they see!
  Then as some loving wife, whose lord has come
Wounded but safe from a far battle home,
Yet must before the day's declining go
On a like quest against another foe,—
With throbbing breast his kingly voice she hears
Her eager gaze is dazzled with her tears,
Nor clearly can she place his tales apart
For the overwhelming passion of her heart,
For joy and love, for pity and for pain,
For thinking "He is come, he goes again!"—
In such confusion of the soul I saw
Their mighty pictures of the vanished Law,

Which, as they held, that Law to Gospel bound
With mystic meaning and design profound:—
Joseph by Dothan and the shepherd's well,
Tobias in the hand of Raphael,—
The crowding people who with joy descry
The food of angels fluttering from the sky;—
Ah, sweet that still upon this earth should be
So many simple souls in holy glee,
Such maids and men, unknowing shame or guile,
Whose whole bright nature beams into a smile!

Thro' all these scenes the fateful story ran,
And the grave presence of the Son of Man:
There was the evening feast, remembered long,
The mystic act and sacramental song;
There was the dreadful garden, rock and tree,
Waker and sleepers in Gethsemane;—
The selfsame forms that I so oft had seen
Shrined the portcullis and the rose between,
When heaven's cold light in cheerless afternoon
Changed while we knelt from sun to ghostly moon.

And one there was who on his deeds could draw
A gaze that half was horror, half was awe,
Who when the supper of the Lord was spread
Drank of the cup and ate the broken bread,
And then, with night without him and within,
Went forth and sinned the unutterable sin.

Better if never on his ways had shone
The Light which is men's life to look upon;
If he had worn a torpid age away
In the poor gains and pleasures of the day,
From toil to toil had been content to go,
Nor ever aim so high or fall so low!

But, when he saw the Christ, he thought to fly
His own base self and selfish misery;
He trusted that before those heavenly eyes
All shameful thoughts were as a dream that dies,
And new life opened on him, great and free,
And love on earth and paradise to be.

But ah! thro' all men some base impulse runs,
(The brute the father and the men the sons,)

Which if one harshly sets him to subdue,
With fiercer insolence it boils anew:
He ends the worst who with best hope began:
How hard is this! how like the lot of man!

    When this man's best desire and highest aim
Had ended in the deed of traitorous shame,
When to his bloodshot eyes grew wild and dim
The stony faces of the Sanhedrim,—
When in his rage he could no longer bear
Men's voices nor the sunlight nor the air,
Nor sleep, nor waking. nor his own quick breath,
Nor God in heaven, nor anything but death,—
I bowed my head, and through my fingers ran
Tears for the end of that Iscariot man,
Lost in the hopeless struggle of the soul
To make the done undone, the broken whole.

    O brother! howsoever, wheresoe'er
Thou hidest now the hell of thy despair,
Hear that one heart can pity, one can know
With thee thy hopeless solitary woe.

But when the treacherous deed was planned and
    done,
The soldiers gathered, and the shame begun,
Thereat the indignant heavens in fierce disdain
Blew down a rushing and uproarious rain;
The tall trees wailed; ill-heard and scarcely seen
Were Jew and Roman those rough gusts between,
Only unmoved one still and towering form
Made, as of old, a silence in the storm.

Then was the cross uplifted; strange to see
That final sign of sad humanity;
For men in childhood for their worship chose
The primal force by which as men they rose;
Then round their homes they bade with boyish grace
The hanging Bacchus swing his comely face;
And now, grown old, they can no more disdain
To look full-front upon the eyes of Pain,
But must all corners of the champaign fill
With bleeding images of this last ill,
Must on yon mountain's pinnacle enshrine
A crucifix, the dead for the divine.

Yet never picture, wonderfully well
By hands of Dürer drawn or Raphael,
Nor wood by shepherds that one art who know
Carved in long nights behind the drifted snow,
Could with such holy sorrows flood and fill
The eyes made glimmering and the heart made still,
As that pale form whose outstretched limbs so long
Made kingship of the infamy of wrong,
O'er whose thorn-twined majestic brows ran down
Blood for anointing from the bitter crown.

Then from the lips of David's Son there brake
Such phrase as David in the Spirit spake,—
Ay, and four words with such a meaning fraught
As seemed an answer to my inmost thought;—
O dreadful cry, and by no seer foreshewn,
"My God, my God, I die and am alone!"

Where is he gone? O men and maidens, where
Is gone the fairest amid all the fair?
Mine eyes desire him, and with dawning day
My heart goes forth to find him on the way.

II.

I, having seen, for certain days apart
Fared with a silent memory at my heart,
And in me great compassion grew for them
Who looked upon that feigned Jerusalem,
For I and all those thousands seemed to be
Like other thousands once in Galilee,
Save that no miracle's divine surprise
Met in the desert our expectant eyes,
No answer calmed our eager hearts enticed
By the mere name and very look of Christ.

So fondly in all ages man will cling
To the least shadow of a Friend and King,
To the faint hope of one to share, to know
The aspiration and the inner woe,—
Forgetting that the several souls of men
Are not like parted drops which meet again
When the tree shakes and to each other run
The kindred crystals glittering into one,—

But like those twin revolving stars which bear
A double solitude thro' the utmost air;
For these, albeit their lit immingled rays
Be living beryl, living chrysoprase,
Tho' burning orb on orb shall whirl and throw
Her amethystine and her golden glow,
Yet must they still their separate pathways keep
And sad procession thro' the eternal deep,
Apart, together, must for ever roll
Round a void centre to an unknown goal.

And thus I mused, and as men's musings will
Come round at last to their own sorrows still,
So mine, who in such words as these began
To mourn the solitary fate of man.

"Thou, Virgil, too, wouldst gladly have been laid
In forest-arches of Thessalian shade,
Or on Laconian lawns have watched all day
The fleet and fair Laconian maidens play,
Till from the rustling of the leaves was shed

Deep sleep upon thy limbs and kingly head,
And Mother Earth diffused with calm control
Peace on her sweetest and her saddest soul.
There 'mid the peasants thou hadst dwelt with joy
The goatherd or the reaper or the boy,
Hadst changed thy fate for theirs, if change could be,
And given for love thy sad supremacy.

"Wert thou not wise, my Master? better far
To live with them and be as these men are;
Better 'mid Phyllis and Lycoris set,—
Their soft eyes darker than the violet,—
With them to smile and sing, for them to bear
The lover's anguish and the fond despair,
Than thus to feel, for ever and forlorn,
The passions set new-risen and die new-born.

"For some men linger in their loves, but I
So soon have finished and so fast go by;
Nay, nor in answering gaze of friends can find
The one soul looking through the double mind:

I love them, but beneath their tenderest tone
This lonely heart is not the less alone;
I love them, but betwixt their souls and me
Are shadowy mountains and a sounding sea.

"Oh heart that oftentimes wouldst gladly win
The whole world's love thy narrow walls within,
Wouldst answer speech with silence, sighs with sighs,
Tears with the effluence of enchanted eyes,—
Then oftentimes in bitterness art fain
To cast that love to the four winds again,
For indignation at the gulfs that bar
For ever soul from soul as star from star!
Sweet are the looks and words, the sigh and kiss,
But can the live soul live by these or this?—
From her sad temple she beholds in vain
The close caresses and the yearning strain;—
Who reaches, who attains her? who has known
Her queenly presence and her tender tone?
What brush has painted, or what song has sung
Her unbetrothèd beauty ever-young?

Only when strange musicians softly play
The ears are glad, and she an hour as they;—
To them the noise is heaven, and to her
A shadowy sweetness and a dying stir.
Ay and sometimes, to such as seek her well,
She in a momentary look can tell
Somewhat of lonely longings, and confess
A fragment of her passion's tenderness.
  Ah, best to rest ere love with worship dies,
Pause at the first encounter of the eyes,
Pass on and dream while yet both souls are free,
'That soul I could have loved, if love could be.'"

  Thus I lamented, and upon me fell
A sense of solitude more sad than hell,
As one forgot, forsaken, and exiled
Of God and man, from woman and from child:—
Hush, hush, my soul, nor let thy speech draw near
That last and incommunicable fear;
All else shall poets sing, but this alone
The man who tells it never can have known.

Thank God! this dizzying and extreme despair
Not one short hour the human heart can bear,
For with that woe the o'erburdened spirit soon
Faints in the dark and fails into a swoon,
The body sickens with the slackening breath,
And the man dies, for this indeed is death.

Lo for each separate soul the Eternal King
Hath separate ways for peace and comforting;
Then pardon if with such intent I tell
The bliss which in my low estate befell:—
For June midnight became the May mid-morn,
In that enchanting home where I was born,
When first the child-heart woke, the child-eyes knew
The bud blush-roses and the sparkling dew.
There gleamed the lake where lone St Herbert saw
The solemn mornings and the soundless awe,—
There were the ferns that shake, the becks that foam,
The Derwent river and the Cumbrian home,—
And there, as once, upon my infant head
His blameless hands the Priest of Nature spread,

AMMERGAU.

Spake fitting words, and gave in great old age
The patriarch's blessing and the bard's presage.
Ah, with what sweet rebuke that vision came!
With how pure hope I called on Wordsworth's name!
O if on earth's green bosom one could lay,
Like him, tired limbs and trustful head, and say,
"To thee, to thee, my mother, I resign
All of my life that still is only mine;
I want no separate pleasures, make me one
With springing seasons in the rain and sun:
To thy great heart our hearts for ever yearn;
Thy children wander, let thy child return!"

To such a man, by self-surrender wise,
With the one soul of all things in his eyes,
To such a life, embosomed and enfurled
In the old unspoken beauty of the world,
Might Nature with a sweet relenting show
More of herself than men by knowledge know;
Till, if he caught the soundless sighing breath
Wherewith the whole creation travaileth,—

If once to human ears revealed could be
The immemorial secret of the sea,—
By such great lessons might that man attain
A life which is not pleasure, is not pain,—
A life collected, elemental, strong,
A sacrosanct tranquillity of song,
Fed by the word unheard, the sight unseen,
The breath that passes man and God between,
When ere the end comes is the end begun,
And the One Soul has flown into the One.

Hereat my soul, which cannot spread for long
Her tethered pinions in the heaven of song,
To her poor home descending with a sigh
Looked through her windows on the earth and sky:
Where she had left the limbs she found them still,
In the same blackness, on the silent hill,
Yet for a while was her return sublime
With dying echoes of the cosmic chime,
And through the parted gloom there fell with her
Some ray from Sire or Son or Comforter;

For in mine ears the silence made a tune,
And to mine eyes the dark was plenilune,
And mountain airs and streams and stones and sod
Bare witness to the Fatherhood of God.

ZÜRICH, *June* 30, 1870.

THE IMPLICIT PROMISE OF IMMORTALITY.

> " Or questi che dall' infima lacuna
> Dell' universo insin qui ha vedute
> Le vite spiritali ad una ad una,
> Supplica a te per grazia di virtute
> Tanto che possa con gli occhi levarsi
> Più alto verso l'ultima salute."
>
> DANTE, *Par.* xxxiii. 22—28.

FRIEND, and it little matters if with thee
In shadowed vales and night's solemnity
Heart has met heart, and soul with soul has known
A deathless kinship and one hope alone;—
Or if thy dear voice by mine ears unheard
Has never spoken me one winged word,
Nor mine eyes seen thee, nor my spirit guessed
The answering spirit hidden in thy breast;—

Known or unknown, seen once and loved for long,
Or only reached by this faint breath of song,
In thine imagined ears I pour again
A faltering message from the man in men,—
Thoughts that are born with summer, but abide
Past summer into sad Allhallowtide.

The world without, men say, the needs within,
Which clash and make what we call sorrow and
    sin,
Tend to adjustment evermore, until
The individual and the cosmic will
Shall coincide, and man content and free
Assume at last his endless empery,
Seeking his Eden and his Heaven no more
By fabled streams behind him or before,
But feeling Pison with Euphrates roll
Round the great garden of his kingly soul.

I answer that, so far, the type that springs
Seems like a race of strangers, not of kings

Less fit for earth, not more so; rather say
Grown like the dog who when musicians play
Feels each false note and howls, while yet the
    true
With doubtful pleasure tremulous thrill him
    through,
Since man's strange thoughts confuse him, and
    destroy
With half-guessed raptures his ancestral joy.

Meantime dim wonder on the untravelled way
Holds our best hearts, and palsies all our day;
One looks on God, and then with eyes struck
    blind
Brings a confusing rumour to mankind;
And others listen, and no work can do
Till they have got that God defined anew;
And in the darkness some have fallen, as fell
To baser gods the folk of Israel,
When with Jehovah's thunders heard too nigh
They wantoned in the shade of Sinai.

Take any of the sons our Age has nursed,
Fed with her food and taught her best and worst;
Suppose no great disaster; look not nigh
On hidden hours of his extremity;
But watch him like the flickering magnet stirred
By each imponderable look and word,
And think how firm a courage every day
He needs to bear him on life's common way,
Since even at the best his spirit moves
Thro' such a tourney of conflicting loves,—
Unwisely sought, untruly called untrue,
Beloved, and hated, and beloved anew;
Till in the changing whirl of praise and blame
He feels himself the same and not the same,
And often, overworn and overwon,
Knows all a dream and wishes all were done.

I know it, such an one these eyes have seen
About the world with his unworldly mien,
And often idly hopeless, often bent
On some tumultuous deed and vehement,

Because his spirit he can nowise fit
To the world's ways and settled rule of it,
But thro' contented thousands travels on
Like a sad heir in disinherison,
And rarely by great thought or brave emprise
Comes out about his life's perplexities,
Looks thro' the rifted cloudland, and sees clear
Fate at his feet and the high God anear.

  Ah let him tarry on those heights, nor dream
Of other founts than that Aonian stream!
Since short and fierce, then hated, drowned,
    and dim
Shall most men's chosen pleasures come to him,—
Not made for such things, nor for long content
With the poor toys of this imprisonment.
Ay, should he sit one afternoon beguiled
By some such joy as makes the wise a child,
Yet if at twilight to his ears shall come
A distant music thro' the city's hum,
So slight a thing as this will wake again

OF IMMORTALITY. 51

The incommunicable homeless pain,
Until his soul so yearns to reunite
With her Prime Source, her Master and Delight,
As if some loadstone drew her, and brain and
  limb
Ached with her struggle to get through to Him.

And is this then delusion? can it be
That like the rest high heaven is phantasy?
Can God's implicit promise be but one
Among so many visions all undone?

Nay, if on earth two souls thro' sundering fate
Can save their sisterhood inviolate,
If dimness and deferment, time and pain,
Have no more lasting power upon those twain
Than stormy thunderclouds which, spent and done,
Leave grateful earth still gazing on the sun,—
If their divine hope gladly can forgo
Such nearness as this wretched flesh can know,
While, spite of all that even themselves may do,

4—2

Each by her own truth feels the other true:—
Faithful no less is God, who having won
Our spirits to His endless unison
Betrays not our dependence, nor can break
The oath unuttered which His silence spake.

Oh dreadful thought, if all our sires and we
Are but foundations of a race to be,—
Stones which one thrusts in earth, and builds
   thereon
A white delight, a Parian Parthenon,
And thither, long thereafter, youth and maid
Seek with glad brows the alabaster shade,
And in processions' pomp together bent
Still interchange their sweet words innocent,—
Not caring that those mighty columns rest
Each on the ruin of a human breast,—
That to the shrine the victor's chariot rolls
Across the anguish of ten thousand souls!

"Well was it that our fathers suffered thus,"

I hear them say, "that all might end in us;
Well was it here and there a bard should feel
Pains premature and hurt that none could heal;
These were their preludes, thus the race began;
So hard a matter was the birth of Man."

And yet these too shall pass and fade and flee,
And in their death shall be as vile as we,
Nor much shall profit with their perfect powers
To have lived a so much sweeter life than ours,
When at the last, with all their bliss gone by,
Like us those glorious creatures come to die,
With far worse woe, far more rebellious strife
Those mighty spirits drink the dregs of life.

Nay, by no cumulative changeful years,
For all our bitter harvesting of tears,
Shalt thou tame man, nor in his breast destroy
The longing for his home which deadens joy;
He cannot mate here, and his cage controls
Safe bodies, separate and sterile souls;

And wouldst thou bless the captives, thou must
   show
The wild green woods which they again shall
   know.

   Therefore have we, while night serenely fell,
Imparadised in sunset's œnomel,
Beheld the empyrean, star on star
Perfecting solemn change and secular,
Each with slow roll and pauseless period
Writing the solitary thoughts of God.
Not blindly in such moments, not in vain,
The open secret flashes on the brain,
As if one almost guessed it, almost knew
Whence we have sailed and voyage whereunto;
Not vainly, for albeit that hour goes by,
And the strange letters perish from the sky,
Yet learn we that a life to us is given
One with the cosmic spectacles of heaven,—
Feel the still soul, for all her questionings,
Parcel and part of sempiternal things;

For us, for all, one overarching dome,
One law the order, and one God the home.

Ah, but who knows in what thin form and strange,
Through what appalled perplexities of change,
Wakes the sad soul, which having once forgone
This earth familiar and her friends thereon
In interstellar void becomes a chill
Outlying fragment of the Master Will;
So severed, so forgetting, shall not she
Lament, immortal, immortality?

If thou wouldst have high God thy soul assure
That she herself shall as herself endure,
Shall in no alien semblance, thine and wise,
Fulfil her and be young in Paradise,
One way I know; forget, forswear, disdain
Thine own best hopes, thine utmost loss and gain,
Till when at last thou scarce rememberest now
If on the earth be such a man as thou,

Nor hast one thought of self-surrender,—no,
For self is none remaining to forgo,—
If ever, then shall strong persuasion fall
That in thy giving thou hast gained thine all,
Given the poor present, gained the boundless
    scope,
And kept thee virgin for the further hope.

This is the hero's temper, and to some
With battle-trumpetings that hour has come,
With guns that thunder and with winds that fall,
With closing fleets and voices augural ;—
For some, methinks, in no less noble wise
Divine prevision kindles in the eyes,
When all base thoughts like frighted harpies flown
In her own beauty leave the soul alone ;
When Love,—not rosy-flushed as he began,
But Love, still Love, the prisoned God in man,—
Shows his face glorious, shakes his banner free,
Cries like a captain for Eternity :—
O halcyon air across the storms of youth,

O trust him, he is true, he is one with Truth!
Nay, is he Christ? I know not; no man knows
The right name of the heavenly Anterôs,—
But here is God, whatever God may be,
And whomsoe'er we worship, this is He.

Ah, friend, I have not said it: who shall tell
In wavering words the hope unspeakable?
Which he who once has known will labour long
To set forth sweetly in persuasive song,
Yea, many hours with hopeless art will try
To save the fair thing that it shall not die,
Then after all despairs, and leaves to-day
A hidden meaning in a nameless lay.

ON ART AS AN AIM IN LIFE.

> "Ein unbegreiflich holdes Sehnen
> Trieb mich, durch Wald und Wiesen hinzugehn,
> Und unter tausend heissen Thränen
> Fühlt' ich mir eine Welt entstehn."—GOETHE.

How was it that he knew it? ay, or where
Beholding an immortal in the air
Fixed he for aye, with swift touch unafraid,
That vision of the vision of a maid,
Whose hands are dropped, whose glowing eyes aspire
To some half-seen concent and heavenly quire,
While at her sacred feet forgotten lie
The useless tools of mortal minstrelsy?

True type of Art, which never long content
Can feed her flame with song or instrument,
Still from the bright supernal dream must draw
Light on her brows, and language, and a law,
If she her glorious message would renew,
Live her great life, and make the picture true,
Where stand that musical sweet maid anear
Saint and evangelist and sage and seer;
They watch Cecilia's eyes, but not for them
Opens on earth the heaven's Jerusalem.

Thou whom with thrills, like the first thrills
    that stir
In a girl's heart when Love is waking her,
With set of soul like the blind strength that sways
Beneath the moon's clear face the watery ways,
God from a child has chosen and set apart
For this one priesthood and last shrine of Art,
See thou maintain thy calling; take no heed
Of such as tell thee there is little need
Of beauty on the earth till peace be here,

That, till some true sun make the world less drear,
All vainly flush in thy thin air withdrawn
Auroral streamers of the untimely dawn.

They err; no other way as yet is known
With God's dim purpose to unite our own,
Except for each to follow as he can
The central impulse that has made him man,
Live his true self, and find his work and rest
In toil or pleasure where that self is best.

And hast thou chosen then? canst thou endure
The purging change of frost and calenture;
Accept the sick recoil, the weary pain
Of senses heightened, keener nerves and brain—
Suffer and love, love much and suffer long—
And live thro' all, and at the last be strong?

For hard the Aonian heights, and far and few
Their starry memories who have won thereto;
Who to the end loved love, who still the same
Followed lifelong the lonely road to fame;

And fame they found, with so great heart had they
Traversed that open unfrequented way.
Have courage; follow; yet no heart have I,
O soul elect, thy pains to prophesy,
Loth to myself to speak them, loth to know
That creatures born for love are born for woe.

Ay, if all else be spared thee, none the less
Enough, enough to bear is loneliness—
The hope that still, till hope with days be done,
Must seek the perfect friend and find not one;
Not one of all whom thine eyes' mastering flame
At will enkindles and at will can tame;—
Not one, O woman, of men strong and free
Whom thy mere presence makes the slaves of thee,
Yet thy king comes not, and the golden door
To thy heart's heart is shut for evermore.

Then oft thy very pulse shall sink away
Sick with the length of disenchanted day,
And after midnight, when the moon looks cold

On lawn and skies grey-azure and grey-gold,
So soft a passion to thy heart shall creep,
To change the dreamful for the dreamless sleep,
That turning round on that unrestful gloom
And peopled silence of thy lonely room,
Thou shalt need all the strength that God can give
Simply to live, my friend, simply to live.

Thou in that hour rejoice, since only thus
Can thy proud heart grow wholly piteous,
Thus only to the world thy speech can flow
Charged with the sad authority of woe
Since no man nurtured in the shade can sing
To a true note our psalm of conquering;
Warriors must chant it, whom our own eyes see
Red from the battle and more bruised than we,
Men who have borne the worst, have known the
    whole,
Have felt the last abeyance of the soul,
Low in the dust with rigid face have lain,
Self-scorned, self-spoiled, self-hated, and self-slain.

ON ART AS AN AIM IN LIFE. 63

Since all alike we bear, but all apart,
One human anguish hidden at the heart,
All with eyes faint, with hopes that half endure,
Seek in the vault our vanished Cynosure,
And strain our helpless oarage, and essay
Thro' flood and fire the innavigable way.

In such dark places truth lies hid, and still
Man's wisdom comes on man against his will,
And his stern sibyl, ere her tale she tell,
Shows the shapes coiling at the gate of hell.

Such be thy sorrows, yet methinks for them
Thine Art herself has help and requiem;
Ah, when some painter, God-encompassed,
Finds the pure passion, lives among the dead,—
When angel eyes regarding thee enthral
Thy spirit in the light angelical,
And heaven and hope and all thy memories seem
Mixed with their being in a lovely dream,—
What place for anger? what to thee is this

That foe and friend judge justly or amiss?
No man can help or harm thee; far away
Their voices sound and like thin air are they;
Thou with the primal Beauty art alone,
And tears forgotten and a world thine own.

How oft Fate's sharpest blows shall leave thee
    strong
With some re-risen ecstasy of song!
How oft the unimagined message bound
In great sonatas and a stormy sound
Shall seize thee and constrain thee, and make
    thee sure
That *this* is true, and *this*, and these endure,—
Being at the root of all things, lying low,
Being Life, and Love, and God has willed it so.

Ah, strange the bond that in one great life
    binds
All master-moments of all master-minds!
Strange the one clan that years nor wars destroy,

The undispersed co-heritage of joy!
Strange that howe'er the sundering ages roll,
From age to age shall soul encounter soul,
Across the dying times, the world's dim roar,
Speak each with each, and live for evermore!

So have I seen in some deep wood divine
The dark and silvery stems of birch and pine;
Apart they sprang, rough earth between them
    lay
Tangled with brambles and with briars, but they
Met at their summits, and a rushing breeze
Inlocked the topmost murmur of the trees.

If only thou to thine own self couldst be
As kind as God and Nature are to thee!
They lade thy bark for nought, they pile thereon
With vain largess the golden cargason,
If with thy royal joys not yet content
Thou needs must lavish all, till all be spent,
If thou wilt change for hurrying loves that die
Thy strength, thine art, thine immortality,—

If thou wilt see thy sweet soul burned like myrrh
Before such gods as have no gift for her.*

For even when once was God well pleased to shed
His thousand glories on a single head,
Amid our baffled lives and struggles dim,
To make one fair and all fair things for him—
Ah, what avail the eyes, the heart of flame,
The angel nature in the angel name?
Amid his fadeless art he fades away
Fair as his pictures but more frail than they,
Leaves deathless shrines, wherein sweet spirits dwell,
But not, not yet, the soul of Raphael.

Yet there are lives that mid the trampling throng
With their prime beauty bloom at evensong,
Souls that with no confusing flutter rise,
Spread their wings once, and sail in Paradise,

* "Tal che tanto ardo che nè mar nè fiume
  Spegner potrian quel foco, ma piace
  Poich' il mio ardor tanto di ben mi face
  Ch' ardendo ognor piu d' arder mi consuma."—RAPHAEL.

Hearts for whom God has judged it best to know
Only by hearsay sin and waste and woe,
Bright to come hither and to travel hence
Bright as they came, and wise in innocence;
So simply fair, so brave and unbeguiled,
Set Christ among the twelve the wiser child.
Wilt thou forget? forget not; keep apart
A certain faithful silence in the heart;
Speak to no friend thereof, and rare and slow
Let thine own thoughts to that their treasure go:—
Ay, an unconscious look, a broken tone,
A soft breath near thee timing with thine own,
These are thy treasures; dearer these to thee
Than the whole store of lifelong memory;
Dearer than joys and passions, for indeed
Those are blown blossoms, this the single seed,
And life is winter for it, death is spring,
And God the sun and heaven the harvesting.

Oh would that life and strength and spirit and song
Could come so flowing, could endure so long,

As might suffice a little at least to praise
The charm and glory of these latter days—
To let the captive thoughts a moment fly
That rise unsummoned and unspoken die!
Oh were I there when oft in some still place
Imagined music flushes in the face,
And silent and sonorous, to and fro,
Thro' the raised head the marching phrases flow!
Were mine the fame, when all the air is fire
With light and life and beauty and desire,
When one, when one thro' all the electric throng
Hurtles the jewel arrows of her song,—
Then crashed from tier on tier, from hand and
    tongue,
The ringing glory makes an old world young!
O marvel, that deep-hid in earth should lie
So many a seed and source of harmony,
Which age on age have slept, and in an hour
Surge in a sea and flame into a flower;
Which are a mystery; which having wist
From his great heart the master-melodist

Strikes till the strong chords tremble and abound
With tyrannous reversion of sweet sound,
Till bar on bar, till quivering string on string,
Break from their maker, are alive and sing,
With force for ever on all hearts to roll
Wave after wave the ocean of his soul!

Yet ah how feeble, ah how faint and low
The organ peals, the silver trumpets blow!
Alas, the glorious thoughts which never yet
Have found a sound in fugue or canzonet,
Nor can the pain of their delight declare
With magic of sweet figures and blue air!
Oh could one once by grace of God disclose
The heart's last sigh, the secret of the rose!
But once set free the soul, and breathe away
Life in the light of one transcendent day!

Not thus has God ordained it; nay, but He
To silent hearts is present silently;

He waits till in thee perish pride and shame,
Sense of thyself, and all thy thoughts of fame;
Then when thy task is over, His begun,
He leads thy soul where all the Arts are one—
Leads to His shrine, and has of old unfurled
To chosen eyes the wonder of the world.
Then let no life but His, no love be near,
Only in thought be even the dearest dear!
No sound or touch must kindle or control
This mounting joy, this sabbath of the soul:
He gives a lonely rapture; ay, as now
From this dark height and Sanminiato's brow,
Watching the beautiful ensanguined day
From Bellosguardo fade and Fiesole,—
Oh look how bridge and river, and dome and spire
Become one glory in the rose-red fire,
Till starlit Arno thro' the vale shall shine
And sweep to sea the roar of Apennine!
This is the spirit's worship: even so
I ween that in a dream and long ago,

Wearing together in her happy hour
The fruit of life and life's enchanting flower,
Herself, alone, essential and divine,
Came his own Florence to the Florentine,
And lily-sceptred in his vision stood
A city like the soul of womanhood.

FLORENCE, *Jan.* 1871.

TWO SISTERS.

First Sister.

When dusk descends and dews begin
   She sees the forest ghostly fair,
And, half in heaven, is drinking in
   The moonlit melancholy air:
The sons of God have charge and care
   Her maiden grace from foes to keep,
And Jesus sends her unaware
   A maiden sanctity of sleep.

Second Sister.

In dreams, in dreams, with sweet surprise
   I see the lord of all these things;
From night and nought with eager eyes
   He comes, and in his coming sings:

TWO SISTERS.

His gentle port is like a king's,
  His open face is free and fair,
And lightly from his brow he flings
  The young abundance of his hair.

First Sister.

Oh who hath watched her kneel to pray
  In hours forgetful of the sun?
Or seen beneath the dome of day
  The hovering seraph seek the nun?
Her weary years at last have won
  A life from life's confusion free:
What else is this but heaven begun,
  Pure peace and simple chastity?

Second Sister.

Oh never yet to mortal maid
  Such sad divine division came
From all that stirs or makes afraid
  The gentle thoughts without a name;

Through all that lives a sacred shame,
A pulse of pleasant trouble, flows,
And tips the daisy's tinge of flame,
And blushes redder in the rose.

First Sister.

From lifted head the golden hair
  Is soft and blowing in the breeze,
And softly on her brows of prayer
  The summer-shadow flits and flees:
Then parts a pathway thro' the trees,
  A vista sunlit and serene,
And there and then it is she sees
  What none but such as she have seen.

Second Sister.

Oh if with him by lea and lawn
  I pressed but once the silvery sod,
And scattered sparkles of the dawn
  From aster and from golden-rod,

I would not tread where others trod,
  Nor dream as other maidens do,
Nor more should need to ask of God,
  When God had brought me thereunto.

SIMMENTHAL.

FAR off the old snows evernew
With silver edges cleft the blue
  Aloft, alone, divine;
The sunny meadows silent slept,
Silence the sombre armies kept,
  The vanguard of the pine.

In that thin air the birds are still,
No ringdove murmurs on the hill
  Nor mating cushat calls;
But gay cicalas singing sprang,
And waters from the forest sang
  The song of waterfalls.

O Fate! a few enchanted hours
Beneath the firs, among the flowers,
  High on the lawn we lay,
Then turned again, contented well,
While bright about us flamed and fell
  The rapture of the day.

And softly with a guileless awe
Beyond the purple lake she saw
  The embattled summits glow;
She saw the glories melt in one,
The round moon rise, while yet the sun
  Was rosy on the snow.

Then like a newly singing bird
The child's soul in her bosom stirred;
  I know not what she sung:—
Because the soft wind caught her hair,
Because the golden moon was fair,
  Because her heart was young.

I would her sweet soul ever may
Look thus from those glad eyes and grey,
    Unfearing, undefiled :
I love her; when her face I see,
Her simple presence wakes in me
    The imperishable child.

ON AN INVALID.

Lo, as the poet finds at will
Than tenderest words a tenderer still
    For one beside him prest;
So from the Lord a mercy flows,
A sweeter balm from Sharon's rose,
    For her that loves him best.

And ere the early throstles stir
With some sweet word from God for her
    The morn returns anew;
For her His face in the east is fair,
For her His breath is in the air,
    His rainbow in the dew.

At such an hour the promise falls
With glory on the narrow walls,
    With strength on failing breath;
There comes a courage in her eyes,
It gathers for the great emprize,
    The deeds of after death.

Albeit thro' this preluding woe
Subdued and softly she must go
    With half her music dumb,
What heavenly hopes to her belong,
And what a rapture, what a song,
    Shall greet His kingdom come!

So climbers by some Alpine mere
Walk very softly thro' the clear
    Unlitten dawn of day:
The morning star before them shows
Beyond the rocks, beyond the snows,
    Their never-travelled way.

Or so, ere singers have begun,
The master-organist has won
    The folk at eve to prayer:
So soft the tune, it only seems
The music of an angel's dreams
    Made audible in air.

But when the mounting treble shakes,
When with a noise the anthem wakes
    A song forgetting sin,—
Thro' all her pipes the organ peals,
With all her voice at last reveals
    The storm of praise within.

The trump! the trump! how pure and high!
How clear the fairy flutes reply!
    How bold the clarions blow!
Nor God Himself has scorned the strain,
But hears it and shall hear again,
    And heard it long ago.

M.

WOULD GOD IT WERE EVENING.

IMPRISONED in the soul and in the sin,
  Imprisoned in the body and the pain,
The accustomed hateful memories within,
  Without the accustomed limbs that ache again :—
Alas! a melancholy peace to win
  With all their notes the nightingales complain,
And I such music as is mine begin,
  Awake for nothing, and alive in vain.
I find few words and falter; then in scorn
My lips are silent; uncreate, unborn,
  Evanishes the visionary lay;
While from clear air upon my soul forlorn
Falls thro' the heedless splendour of the morn
  A sadness as the sadness of to-day.

WOULD GOD IT WERE MORNING.

My God, how many times ere I be dead
    Must I the bitterness of dying know?
How often like a corpse upon my bed
    Compose me and surrender me and so
Thro' hateful hours and ill-remembered
    Between the twilight and the twilight go
By visions bodiless obscurely led
    Thro' many a wild enormity of woe?
And yet I know not but that this is worst
When with that light, the feeble and the first,
    I start and gaze into the world again,
And gazing find it as of old accurst
And grey and blinded with the stormy burst
    And blank appalling solitude of rain.

HIGH TIDE AT MIDNIGHT.

No breath is on the glimmering ocean-floor,
    No blast beneath the windless Pleiades,
But thro' dead night a melancholy roar,
    A voice of moving and of marching seas,—
The boom of thundering waters on the shore
    Sworn with slow force by desolate degrees
Once to go on, and whelm for evermore
    Earth and her folk and all their phantasies.
Then half-asleep in the great sound I seem
Lost in the starlight, dying in a dream
    Where overmastering Powers abolish me,—
Drown, and thro' dim euthanasy redeem
My merged life in the living ocean-stream
    And soul environing of shadowy sea.

ON A GRAVE AT GRINDELWALD.

HERE let us leave him; for his shroud the snow,
   For funeral-lamps he has the planets seven,
For a great sign the icy stair shall go
   Between the heights to heaven.

One moment stood he as the angels stand,
   High in the stainless eminence of air;
The next, he was not, to his fatherland
   Translated unaware.

AFTER AN INTERVIEW.

So while the careless crowd have gazed and gone
  Sits one man stedfast in a chosen place,
And of all faces which they gaze upon
  Desires one only face:

For early morning finds the lover there,
  Also at eventide his eyes are dim,
Till at the last he slowly is aware
  His soul has flown from him.

So also he whom vanished organ-lays
  Have stung to jubilance and thrilled to tears
Sits with sonorous memories of praise
  Tranced in his echoing ears:

Thro' all his blood the billowy clangours roll,
Thro' all his body leaps the living strain,
And sweetly, stilly, in his hidden soul
    The soft notes sink again.

Then while the trooping singers outward range
    He waits enthralled in that superb surprise:
Like airy ghosts they pass him by, nor change
    His wide and wistful eyes.

So stays he in high heaven a little space,
    Then treads the portal which the others trod,
And issues into silence, face to face
    With darkness and with God.

LOVE AND FAITH.

Lo if a man, magnanimous and tender,
  Lo if a woman, desperate and true,
Make the irrevocable sweet surrender,
  Show to each other what the Lord can do,—

Each, as I know, a helping and a healing,
  Each to the other strangely a surprise,
Heart to the heart its mystery revealing,
  Soul to the soul in melancholy eyes,—

Where wilt thou find a riving or a rending
  Able to sever them in twain again?
God hath begun, and God's shall be the ending,
  Safe in His bosom and aloof from men.

Her thou mayest separate but shalt not sunder,
    Tho' thou distress her for a little while ;—
Rapt in a worship, ravished in a wonder,
    Stayed on the stedfast promise of a smile,

Scarcely she knoweth if his arms have found her—
    Waves of his breath make tremulous the air—
Or if the thrill within her and around her
    Be but the distant echo of his prayer.

Nay, and much more ; for love in his demanding
    Will not be bound in limits of our breath,
Calls her to follow where she sees him standing
    Fairer and stronger for the plunge of death ;—

Waketh a vision and a voice within her
    Sweeter than dreams and clearer than complaint,
" Is it a man thou lovest, and a sinner?
    No! but a soul, o woman, and a saint!"

Well,—if to her such prophecy be given,
    Strong to illuminate when sight is dim,
Then tho' my Lord be holy in the heaven
    How should the heavens sunder me from Him?

She and her love,—how dimly has she seen him
    Dark in a dream and windy in a wraith!
I and my Lord,—between me and between Him
    Rises the lucent ladder of my faith.

Ay, and thereon, descending and ascending,
    Suns at my side and starry in the air,
Angels, His ministers, their tasks are blending,
    Bear me the blessing, render Him the prayer.

A PRAYER.

O FOR one minute hark what we are saying!
　This is not pleasure that we ask of Thee!
Nay, let all life be weary with our praying,
　Streaming of tears and bending of the knee :—

Only we ask thro' shadows of the valley
　Stay of thy staff and guiding of thy rod,
Only, when rulers of the darkness rally,
　Be thou beside us, very near, O God!

A LAST APPEAL.

O SOMEWHERE, somewhere, God unknown,
  Exist and be!
I am dying; I am all alone;
  I must have Thee!

God! God! my sense, my soul, my all,
  Dies in the cry:—
Saw'st thou the faint star flame and fall?
  Ah! it was I.

TENERIFFE.

I.

ATLANTID islands, phantom-fair,
   Throned on the solitary seas,
Immersed in amethystine air,
   Haunt of Hesperides!
Farewell! I leave Madeira thus
Drowned in a sunset glorious,
The Holy Harbour fading far
Beneath a blaze of cinnabar.

II.

What sights had burning eve to show
   From Tacoronte's orange-bowers,
From palmy headlands of Ycod,
   From Orotava's flowers!

When Palma or Canary lay
Cloud-cinctured in the crimson day,—
Sea, and sea-wrack, and rising higher
Those purple peaks 'twixt cloud and fire.

III.

But oh the cone aloft and clear
   Where Atlas in the heavens withdrawn
To hemisphere and hemisphere
   Disparts the dark and dawn!
O vaporous waves that roll and press!
Fire-opalescent wilderness!
O pathway by the sunbeams ploughed
Betwixt those pouring walls of cloud!

IV.

We watched adown that glade of fire
   Celestial Iris floating free;
We saw the cloudlets keep in choir
   Their dances on the sea;

The scarlet, huge, and quivering sun
Feared his due hour was overrun,—
On us the last he blazed, and hurled
His glory on Columbus' world.

V.

Then ere our eyes the change could tell,
  Or feet bewildered turn again,
From Teneriffe the darkness fell
  Head-foremost on the main :—
A hundred leagues was seaward thrown
The gloom of Teyde's towering cone,—
Full half the height of heaven's blue
That monstrous shadow overflew.

VI.

Then all is twilight; pile on pile
  The scattered flocks of cloudland close,
An alabaster wall, erewhile
  Much redder than the rose !—

Falls like a sleep on souls forspent
Majestic Night's abandonment;
Wakes like a waking life afar
Hung o'er the sea one eastern star.

VII.

O Nature's glory, Nature's youth,
   Perfected sempiternal whole!
And is the World's in very truth
   An impercipient Soul?
Or doth that Spirit, past our ken,
Live a profounder life than men,
Awaits our passing days, and thus
In secret places calls to us?

VIII.

O fear not thou, whate'er befall
   Thy transient individual breath;—
Behold, thou knowest not at all
   What kind of thing is Death:

And here indeed might Death be fair,
If Death be dying into air,—
If souls evanished mix with thee,
Illumined Heaven, eternal Sea.

1874.

A LETTER FROM NEWPORT.

φαίη κ' ἀθανάτους καὶ ἀγήρως ἔμμεναι αἰεὶ
ὅς τότ' ἐπαντιάσει' ὅτ' Ἰάονες ἄθροοι εἶεν.

THE crimson leafage fires the lawn,
  The piled hydrangeas blazing glow;
How blue the vault of breezy dawn
  Illumes the Atlantic's crested snow!
'Twixt sea and sands how fair to ride
  Through whispering airs a starlit way,
And watch those flashing towers divide
  Heaven's darkness from the darkling bay!

Ah, friend, how vain their pedant's part,
  Their hurrying toils how idly spent,
How have they wronged the gentler heart
  Which thrills the awakening continent,

Who have not learnt on this bright shore
 What sweetness issues from the strong,
Where flowerless forest, cataract-roar,
 Have found a blossom and a song!

Ah, what imperial force of fate
 Links our one race in high emprize!
Nor aught henceforth can separate
 Those glories mingling as they rise;
For one in heart, as one in speech,
 At last have Child and Mother grown,—
Fair Figures! honouring each in each
 A beauty kindred with her own.

Through English eyes more calmly soft
 Looks from grey deeps the appealing charm;
Reddens on English cheeks more oft
 The rose of innocent alarm:—
Our old-world heart more gravely feels,
 Has learnt more force, more self-control;
For us through sterner music peals
 The full accord of soul and soul.

But ah, the life, the smile untaught,
    The floating presence feathery-fair!
The eyes and aspect that have caught
    The brilliance of Columbian air!
No oriole through the forest flits
    More sheeny-plumed, more gay and free;
On no nymph's marble forehead sits
    Proudlier a glad virginity.

So once the Egyptian, gravely bold,
    Wandered the Ionian folk among,
Heard from their high Letôon rolled
    That song the Delian maidens sung;
Danced in his eyes the dazzling gold,
    For with his voice the tears had sprung,—
"They die not, these! they wax not old,
    They are ever-living, ever-young!"

Spread then, great land! thine arms afar,
    Thy golden harvest westward roll;
Banner with banner, star with star,
    Ally the tropics and the pole;—

There glows no gem than these more bright
  From ice to fire, from sea to sea;
Blossoms no fairer flower to light
  Through all thine endless empery.

And thou come hither, friend! thou too
  Their kingdom enter as a boy;
Fed with their glorious youth renew
  Thy dimmed prerogative of joy:—
Come with small question, little thought,
  Through thy worn veins what pulse shall flow,
With what regrets, what fancies fraught,
  Shall silver-footed summer go:—

If round one fairest face shall meet
  Those many dreams of many fair,
And wandering homage seek the feet
  Of one sweet queen, and linger there;
Or if strange winds betwixt be driven,
  Unvoyageable oceans foam,
Nor this new earth, this airy heaven,
  For thy sad heart can find a home.

NEWPORT, R. I., *Sept.*, 1879.

EPITHALAMIUM.

To him our wisest, him our best,
    What praise or guerdon could we bring?
What crown of ours could show confest
    Our crownless unanointed king?—
Our hearts we gave him; strong and true
    His heart replied, to help or heal,
Yet dumbly in his look we knew
    A nameless infinite appeal.

Wealth, honours, fame,—hope's common range,—
    We named and smiled and passed them by:—
No shine or shade without could change
    The vision of that inward eye.

That temple by great thoughts upbuilt
  Was void and stedfast, cold and fair;
No wine was on its altar spilt,
  A god unknown was worshipped there.

Yet rarely thro' its heights he heard
  Egerian echoes floating free;
An unbeholden presence stirred
  His brow's austere serenity.
Then from the altar flashed the flame,
  Flowed on the hearth the fervid wine,—
From heaven and air the answer came
  And stood a Spirit in the shrine.

One voice alone, one only hand,
  The immaterial gift could give,
Could bid the world-wide soul expand,
  A heart within the great heart live:—
No word of praise she sought to say,
  For him no worldly crown to win,
But with a look, and in a day,
  She gave a kingdom from within.

EPITHALAMIUM.

O fate ordained, august, secure,
    And Love the child that never dies,
When to the stainless earth is pure
    And life all wisdom to the wise!
Aye shall the inner hope endure
    That looks from their illumined eyes;
Thro' this the very world stands sure,
    And souls like these are Paradise.

STANZAS ON SHELLEY.

OH, not like ours that life was born,
    No mortal mother Shelley knew,
But kindled by some starry morn
    Lit like a snow-flake from the blue;
Saw on some peak the lightnings gleam,
    The lingering soft auroras play;
Then foamlike on a leaping stream
    Sped downwards to the earthly day.

So keen a wish had winged his flight—
    His heart was faint with such desire—
To bear from that supernal light
    A Promethèan fount of fire:

His quivering thyrsus flashed with flame,
　He sang the spell long learnt above;
With ardent eyes one only name
　He named; the mountains echoed "Love!"

But ah! for men no healing wrought
　That spell, that spirit's angel bloom:
Close, close about him frowned and fought
　Their words of anger, looks of gloom:
Gloomed overhead the iron reign
　Of stifling custom, hates that kill;
From Earth's dark places sighed in vain
　Her old immedicable ill.

"And yet methinks one soul might know
　The bliss unknown, the tale untold!
One heart might melt in mine, and so
　For twain at least the age be gold!"
He called;—and ah! what mortal maid
　Had heard unmoved that seraph tongue?
What Daphne lingered in her shade
　When that unstained Apollo sung?

But oft in vain shall love be given
  When mighty spirits mourn alone;
Too rarely, rarely falls from heaven
  A woman-heart to match their own:
He saw his Vision smile in sleep,
  And close she seemed, and floated far;
Life-long across life's darkling deep
  He chased that image of a star.

Yet, with an Orphic whisper blent,
  A Spirit in the west-wind sighs;
Gaze from the conscious firmament
  Some God's unfathomable eyes:
He saw, he felt them: "Thou be mine,
  As I am thine, thou primal whole!
Ye elements, my life enshrine,
  Enfold, entomb me, soul in soul!"

He called; they heard him; high in air
  The impetuous Winds came whirling free;
Dashed on his brow, swept through his hair
  Untamed caresses of the Sea;

The Fire up-leapt in ardent birth
To her thin substance his to win;
That heart of hearts the dædal Earth,
Her own unfolding, drew therein.

IN HENRY VII.'s CHAPEL,
WESTMINSTER ABBEY.

O HOLY heart of England! inmost shrine
    Of Mary's grace divine;
Proud aisles, where all things noble, all things high,
    Her sweet soul magnify;
Vaults where the bones of mighty kings are laid,
    Blest by a Mother-Maid!
One heart, great shrine, thou knewest then, be sure,
    As thine own Mistress pure;
Eyes that like hers by supplication bless,
    And reign by lowliness.

Oh solemn hour, and on Love's altar sent
    Sun-fire for sacrament,
When in the age-old answers she and I
    Made each to each reply;—
Ay, for a moment rose and were alone
    With Him who was our own,
While wide on earth heaven's height made luminous
    Shone, and the Lord on us.
O Priest, whose voice from that irradiant sun
    Proclaimed the twain made one,—
Amid the banners of his Order spake
    That oath no age can break!
Voice of a Ruler born to soothe and sway
    Man on his wandering way,
Dowered with the courage glad, the wisdom mild,
    Which keep the sage a child;
Whose high thoughts immanent have built him fair
    A shrine in the upper air
Stainless, and still, and ever oftener trod
    By messengers of God!

While to that voice amid those memories heard
    Answered her underword,
No wonder if the Eternal Presence then
    Seemed mute no more to men,
Nor gulf betwixt, nor any darkness shed
    On souls miscalled the dead;
Since we and they, henceforth or long ago,
    One life alone can know;—
Since from seas under earth to stars above
    There is no joy but love,
Nor in God's house shall any glory be
    Save God and such as she.

STANZAS

ON MR WATTS' COLLECTED WORKS.

"Elysian beauty, melancholy grace,
Brought from a pensive, though a happy place."

I.

FOR many a year the master wrought,
 And wisdom deepened slow with years;
Guest-chambers of his inmost thought
 Were filled with shapes too stern for tears;—
Yet Joy was there, and murmuring Love,
 And Youth that hears with hastened breath,
But, throned in peace all these above,
 The unrevealing eyes of Death.

II.

Faces there were which won him yet,
 Fair daughters of an iron age:
In iron truth pourtrayed he set
 Warrior and statesman, bard and sage.
From hidden deeps their past he drew,
 The ancestral bent of stock and stem;
More of their hearts than yet they knew
 Thro' their own gaze looked out on them.

III.

Yet oftenest in the past he walked,
 With god or hero long gone by,
Oft, like his pictured Genius, talked
 With rainbow forms that span the sky:
Thereto his soul hath listed long,
 When silent voices spake in air,—
Hath mirrored many an old-world song
 Remote and mystic, sad and fair.

M.

IV.

For here the Thracian, vainly wise,
　Close on the light his love has led;—
Oh hearken! her melodious cries
　Fade in the mutter of the dead:—
"Farewell! from thy embrace I pass,
　Drawn to the formless dark alone:
I stretch my hands,—too weak, alas!
　And I no more, no more thine own."

V.

And here is she whom Art aflame
　Smote from the rock a breathing maid;
Calm at the fiery call she came,
　Looked on her lover unafraid;
Nor quite was sure if life were best,
　And love, till love with life had flown,
Or still with things unborn to rest,
　Ideal beauty, changeless stone.

VI.

Ah! which the sweeter? she who stands,
  A soul to woe that moment born,—
Regretfully her aimless hands
  Drooping by Psyche's side forlorn?—
Woke with a shock the god unknown,
  And sighing flushed, and flying sighed:
Grey in the dawning stands alone
  His desolate and childly bride.

VII.

Or she whose soft limbs swiftly sped
  The touch of very gods must shun,
And, drowned in many a boscage, fled
  The imperious kisses of the sun?
Mix, mix with Daphne, branch and frond,
  O laurel-wildness, laurel-shade!
Let Nature's life,—no love beyond,—
  Make all the marriage of the maid!

VIII.

Or she who, deep in Latmian trees,
  Stoops from the height her silver sheen?
Dreams in a dream her shepherd sees
  The crescent car, the bending queen.
One kiss she gives; the Fates refuse
  A closer bond or longer stay:
The boy sleeps still; her orb renews
  Its echoless unmated way.

IX.

All these some hope unanswered know,
  Some laws that prison, fates that bar;
Baffled their spirit-fountains flow
  Toward things diviner and afar.
Such dole at heart their painter felt,
  Within, without, such sights to see;
Who in our monstrous London dwelt,
  And half remembered Arcady.

X.

Ah, sure, those springs of joy and pain
  By some remote recall are stirred;
His ancient Guardians smile again,
  And touch a colour, speak a word.
Not all asleep thy gods of Greece
  Lie tumbled on the Coan shore:—
O painter! thou that knew'st their peace
  Must half remember evermore!

XI.

So gazed on Phidias' Warrior-maid,
  Methinks, Ægina's kingly boy:—
She stood, her Gorgon shield displayed,
  Too great for love, too grave for joy.
All day her image held him there;
  This world, this life, with day grew dim;
Some glimmering of the Primal Fair
  Pre-natal memories woke in him.

XII.

Then as he walked, like one who dreamed,
　Thro' silent highways silver-hoar,
More wonderful that city seemed,
　And he diviner than before :—
A voice was calling, All is well ;
　Clear in the vault Selene shone,
And over Plato's homestead fell
　The shadow of the Parthenon.

PART II.

THE PASSING OF YOUTH.

ARGUMENT.

REFLECTIONS in the Campo Santo at Pisa. The fresco, ascribed to Orcagna, which represents Death at the Festival, suggests the thought that it may be better to die in the flush of youth than to live on into a state of decadence and disgust with life (1—30). He who thus feels the freshness of youth escaping him cannot renew it by the mere contact with the fresh emotion of others (31—58). His habitual melancholy contrasts painfully with the accesses of grief which alternated with keen joy in his earlier years (59—92). If he now occasionally fancies that the old power of feeling remains to him, the illusion does not last long, and he is fain to acquiesce in the exhaustion of his emotional power (93—114). Yet he can scarcely avoid bitterness at the thought of how small his share of emotional delight has been in comparison with all that the future holds in reserve for mankind (115—146). Sometimes he will shape a vision of some ideal love which might have been his, though well knowing that even should some one be born into the world who realizes his dream he will have no part in her affections or memories (147—176). Instinctively revolting at the prospect of an approaching extinction he reviews with alternations of hope and despair the possibility of a future existence (177—222). Light on this subject often seems as unattainable now as in the days when Virgil pondered the same problems (223—240). But certain moments seem to carry with them something of inspired insight or of lofty emotion which is at any rate the best basis for practice (241—290). At any rate a man by the sheer effort of the Will may maintain himself in that state of inflexible fearlessness which Virgil admires in Lucretius (291—296). The languor and melancholy which the aspect of Pisa symbolises may be overcome by this resolute courage, this 'living force of the mind' which Lucretius found strong enough to afford to mankind at least the triumph of intellectual insight and philosophic calm (297—312).

THE PASSING OF YOUTH.

ERGO VIVIDA VIS ANIMI PERVICIT—

AT Pisa, where the cypress-spires alway
Stand in the languor of the Pisan day,
And airs are motionless, and Arno fills
With brimming hush the hollow of the hills ;—
There once alone, from noon till evening's shade,
I paced the echoing cloistral colonnade ;
Heard like a dream the grey rain-river fall
On hallowed turf that hath the end of all ;
Saw like a ghost the flying form that saith,
" Orcagna knew me ; know me ; I am Death." 10

Come then, I said, kind Death, come ever thus,
Swift with a sword on young men amorous!

And thou, youth, thank her that her wiry wings
Snatch thee full-blooded from the feast of kings;
Nor live to outlive thyself, to sigh and know
With waxing restlessness a waning glow;
Even from those hateful ashes of desire
To feel reborn the cold and fruitless fire;
To look, and long a little, and turn aside,
Half over-satiate, half unsatisfied.   20
Then is no help but that thine eyes must see
Thine inner self stand forth and mock at thee;
Must watch to death in shadowy convoy roll
Thy strength, thy song, thy beauty and thy soul.
No help! and with what anger shalt thou then
Look on the glad lives of up-springing men,
With hearts still high, and still before them fair
All oceans navigable and ambient air;—
How shalt thou love, and envy, and despise
Their hope unreasonable and ardent eyes!   30

Then if some stainless maid desires no more
Than her fresh soul into thy soul to pour,—

THE PASSING OF YOUTH.

All her pure glory at thy feet will fling,
And give thee youth and ask not anything;—
Take not the boon illusive;—yet I know
That thou wilt take and she will have it so;
Nor once alone; but thou in vain shalt see
On many a cheek the rose of amity,
And for no lasting profit shalt essay
On many a heart thy mastering wistful way, 40
And speak thus gently, and regard her thus
With loving eyes a little tyrannous,—
As though her passion passion's power could give,
Or heart could melt in heart, or death could live.

Alas, in vain shall that love-light illume
Her cheek transparent and her rosy bloom,
And hopes that flush and happy thoughts that rise
Make living lucid sapphire of her eyes;—
Since all is nothing, and aloof, alone,
With swirl and severance as of Arve and Rhone, 50
Must heart from heart dissunder; way from way
Part, and to-morrow know not of to-day.

So weighs the Past upon us; such a thing
It is to have grown too wise for comforting;
In a few notes to have sung all thy song,
And in a few years to have lived too long;
Till thy mere voice and soulless shadow now
Recall that this was thine, and this was thou.

O sweet young hours, when one divine love yet
Seemed a new birth thou never couldst forget! 60
When day on day for the impassioned boy
Came flooding like a silver sea of joy,—
So keen that often o'er his eyes would sweep
The gracious wings of momentary sleep,
To leave their light re-risen, and the brain
Re-kindled for the rapture that was pain!
 Then griefs wherein no thought of self had part,
The just and manful angers of the heart,—
When hands would clench, and clear cheek light and glow,
To be so powerless for another's woe,   70

And young disdain, and love, and generous fears
Burst in a proud simplicity of tears!

Ah! even those pains were noble! strange and
  pure
As thunders of the breaking calenture,
When storm-refreshed the bounding rivers run,
And the oak shakes his diamonds in the sun,
Nor cares how brightly on the forest flew
That wildering levin-bolt alive anew.
But these succeeding sorrows I compare
To the chill ruin of October air,   80
When all earth's life is spent, nor can regain
Strength in the hopeless pauses of the rain,
But scarce the dumb woods shiver, and at a breath
Falls the wan leaf, and then they whisper, 'Death.'

For faiths will die and ancient landmarks fail,
And promised Eden grow a lovely tale;
And even, by length of years, by sheer decay,
The fiery flower of Love consumes away;

No help to seek, and none to blame, but gone
Like all things else that men set life upon; 90
Like all that seemed immortal, all that smiled
Mixt with the morn and glory of the child.

Then one at last in cities far away
Hears late in night lamenting hautboys play,
Sees glittering all in swan-soft order sit
That kingdom's fairest and the pride of it;
Till, when one face amid all faces seems
Lit with the witchery of a thousand dreams,
He wonders,—could he change his race and tongue,
And once be joyous, and again be young,— 100
If, leaning o'er that braided golden head,
New words and sweeter he should find unsaid,
And a last secret and pervading stir
In the soft look and woman-ways of her.
Nay, the fond dream he would so fain prolong
Breaks with a shock of intermitting song,
And truth returns, and in a single sigh
Must that faint love be born at once and die.

'For soon,' he saith, 'will feverous dreams be
   spent;
Exhaustion surely shall beget content;   110
I have lost my battle; doubtless it is best
To have no longing left me but for rest;
In this worn heart, with some last love's decease,
To make a solitude and call it peace.'

Yet when a wave of happy laughter low
Stirs in his soul the deep of long ago;—
When his world-wearied ears have overheard
From sweet new lips a sweet accustomed word;—
Then all awakes again, and worse than nought
Seem the best passions which his youth has
   brought,—   120
Being such a drop in so profound a sea,
Having given one glimpse of Love's supremacy,
Shown at a glance what great delight shall come
When his eyes see not and his lips are dumb.
How many a glorious joy for ever missed!
How many words unspoken, lips unkissed!

Eyes that shall yet renew with softer play
Thro' many a century the world-old way;—
Hearts from whose glow shall glory of love be shed
Round hearts still living, and o'er his tomb long
 dead!

Man, while thou mayst, love on! with sound
 and flowers
Make maddening moments into maddening hours,
Let hours aflame enkindle as they fly
Those loves of yore that in thy darkness die:—
Blest, in that glamour could all life be spent
Before the dawn and disillusionment!
Love on! thy far-off children shall possess
That flying gleam of rainbow happiness:—
Each wish unfilled, impracticable plan,
Goes to the forging of the force of Man;
Thro' thy blind craving novel powers they gain,
And the slow Race developes in its pain:—
See their new joy begotten of thy woe,
When what thy soul desired their soul shall know;—

THE PASSING OF YOUTH.

Thy heights unclimbed shall be their wonted way,
Thy hope their memory, and thy dream their day.

Ah, but I had a vision once, nor dare
Recall it often, lest it melt in air!
Whose was the face that thro' the shadows came
And shook the dew from hair that waved like flame? 150
What made her look aërial? ay, or shed
Divineness on that visionary head?
And whence the words that on her silence hung,
Looked thro' her eyes and died upon her tongue?—
'Love, who had dreamt it, who had dared to say
Our bliss could come so close, and flee away?'

Not even the Night shall know her; it may be
Some falling star would speak it to the sea;
Then the sea's voice would to the shore declare
The hidden sweetness of the First and Fair, 160
And fisher-maidens into morn prolong
For love the amorous echoes of the song.

Yet if indeed that dear face fugitive,
The dream-begotten, in the day shall live,
And through night's spaces floats the lovely shade
Before the birth and body of the maid,—
How sweet it were to die and still be strong,
To clasp her close with grave and mastering
    song,—
That she with no interpreter might see
The sincere man and hidden heart of thee,   170
And down her soft cheek happy tears might roll,
Hearing the dead voice of the sister-soul!
    How slight and how impossible a boon
I ask, and love too late, or live too soon!
Only the brief regret, the grace of sighs,
I ask; can Fate deny it? Fate denies.

    Crushed, as by following wave the wave before!
To have lived and loved so little, and live no more!
Call this not sleep; through sweet sleep's longest
    scope
Runs in a golden dream unconscious Hope; 180

Hope parts the lips and stirs the happy breath,
And sleep is sleep, but endless Death is Death.

Hereat the soul will evermore recur
To that great chance which makes herself for
    her;
If but the least light glimmer and least hope glow
From that unseen place which no soul can know,—
Whereof so many a sage hath spun in vain
Thoughts fancy-fashioned in a dreaming brain;—
Whereof the priests, for all they say and sing,
Know none the more, nor help in anything;— 190
Nor more herein can man to man avail
Than to his sorrowing mate the nightingale,—
Nor more can brother unto brother tell
Than blind who leads the blind, though loving
    well :—
If by some gleam unearthly indeed be lit
That land, and God the sun and moon of it,—
How easy then, how possible to bear
The thoughts that come at night, and are despair,—

THE PASSING OF YOUTH.

Youth wasted, hopes decaying, friends untrue,
Life with no faith to follow or deed to do;   200
Loves lost, and waning joys, and waked again
The old unquenchable relapse of pain;—
And through these all the ceaseless fruitless fire,
The upward heavenward flickering fierce desire,
The thrilling pang, the tremor of unrest,
The quickening God unborn within the breast,
Which none believe but who have felt, and they
Feel evermore by night and in the day;
For tho' in early youth such longing rose
This single passion gathers as it goes;   210
And this at dawn wakes with thee, this at even
Hangs in the kindling canopies of heaven;
This, like a hidden water's running tune
Revives the wistful pause of afternoon;—
For strength is this and weakness, hope and fear
By turns, as far sometimes, sometimes anear,
Glows the great Hope, which all too oft will seem
A false inherited delightful dream,

Dreamt of our fathers for blind ease, which we
Knowing that they knew not, seeing they could not
    see,   220
Must wake from and have done with, and be brave
Without a heaven to hope or God to save.

    O sighs that strongly from my bosom flew!
O heart's oblation sacrificed anew!
O groans and tears of all men and of mine!
O many midnights prostrate and supine,
Unbearable and profitless, and spent
For the empty furtherance of a vain intent,—
From God or Nothingness, from Heaven or Hell,
To wrest the secret that they would not tell,— 230
To grasp a life beyond life's shrinking span
And learn at last the chief concerns of man!

    O last last hope when all the rest are flown!
O one thing worth the knowing, and still unknown!
O sought so passionately and found no more
To-day than when the sad voice sang of yore,

How 'God the innumerous souls in great array
To Lethe summons by a wondrous way,
Till these therein their ancient pain forgive,
Forget their life, and will again to live.' 240

Yet in some hours when earth and heaven are
   fair,
In some sabbatical repose of air,
When all has passed that dizzied or defiled,
And thy clear soul comes to thee as a child,
Then incorruptible, unending, free,
Like the moon's golden road upon the sea,
The light of life on unbewildered eyes
A moment dawns, and in a moment dies.

So dimly glad may some lone heart recall
Perchance a magic end of evenfall, 250
When far on misty fells the moon has made
An argent fleece, and neither shine nor shade;
Hills beyond hills she silvers as she sails,
Hills beyond hills, and valleys in the vales;

Till they that float and watch her scarcely feel
The liquid darkness tremble at the keel,
Beholding scarce behold her, hardly dare
To look one look through that enchanted air,
Lest some unknown God should no longer hide
His glory from his creatures glorified,   260
Should shine too manifest, too soon display
To eyes that dream the immeasurable day.

Remember; I remember; hast not thou
Hours in the past more living than all life now?
One hour, perchance, that thro' the hush of fate
In shadowy veil came to thee consecrate,
Known without knowledge, felt without a name,—
And life brings other hours, but not the same?

This, then, was revelation; this shall be
Thy crown of youth and star of memory;   270
Strong in this strength the ennobled years shall
    run,
And life grow single and thy will be one:—

Ay, like great passages in order played
Shall changeful life grow one and unafraid;—
For these are one in many, and tho' sometimes
The bell-like melodising rings and rhymes,
And warbles such a whisper now and then,
Too sweet, and scarce endurable to men,
Yet on thro' all the tune returns the same,
Embattled resonance, a flooding flame, 280
And dies to live again, and wins, and still
Rules the great notes and sways them as it will:—
Thus let thy life thro' all adventure go,
And keep it masterful, and save it so;—
Not reared too separate nor lulled too long
By the incommunicable trance of song,
Nor over-amorous, nay, nor overset
Too sweetly by the fain and fond regret,
The after-thought of kisses, and the tear
For loves whom day disparts and dreams bring
 near. 290
Since what man is man knows not, but he knows
That his one will is like a trump that blows;—

While breath is in him it can clarion well,
Heaven-sweet, and heard above the roar of hell;
Ay, 'Fate and Fear beneath his feet are thrown,
All Fears and Fates, and Hell's insatiate moan.'

Then, Pisa, let thy sullen airs o'erhead
Lull that unaltering city of the dead;
Let swimming Arno, hushed at last like thee,
Draw to his doom and gather to the sea;   300
Fold upon fold let rainy evening roll,
And thy deep bells strike death upon the soul;—
There is a courage that from need began,
And grows with will, and is at last the man;
Which on thro' storm, thro' darkness, thro' despair,
Hopes, and will hope, and dares, and still can dare;
And this is Virtue; and thou canst not bind
O Death, this 'living spirit of the mind,'
Which 'far aloof,' the Roman verses say,
'Holds an unseen illimitable way;   310
Far, far aloof can sail with wings unfurled
Beyond the flaming rampire of the world.'

1871-2.

SWEET SEVENTEEN.

I KNEW a maid.; her form and face
    Were lily-slender, lily-fair;
Hers was a wild unconscious grace,
    A ruddy-golden crown of hair.

Thro' those child-eyes unchecked, untamed,
    The happy thoughts transparent flew,
Yet some pathetic touch had tamed
    To gentler grey their Irish blue.

So from her oak a Dryad leant
    To look, with wondering glance and gay,
Where Jove, uncrowned and kingly, went
    With Maia down the woodland way.

Their glory lit the amorous air;
  The golden touched the Olympian head;
But Zephyr o'er Cyllene bare
  That secret the Immortals said.

The nymph they saw not, passing nigh;
  She melted in her leafy screen;
But from the boughs that seemed to sigh
  A dewdrop trembled on the green.

That nymph her oak for aye must hold;
  The girl has life and hope, and she
Shall hear one day the secret told,
  And roam herself in Arcady.

I see her still; her cheek aglow,
  Her gaze upon the future bent;
As one who through the world will go
  Beloved, bewitching, innocent.

AH, no more questions, no more fears,
    But let us at the end have rest;
Shed if thou wilt the unfallen tears,
    But shed them on my breast.
Who guesses what the unfathomed years
    May bear of life and love and woe?
Not in our eyes nor to our ears
    Those things are plain to know.

We only feel that side by side
    Each loving shoulder leans on each,
With looks too precious to divide
    By fragmentary speech.
Nor this nor aught can long abide,
    But passes, passes like to-day,
Till each shall fare without a guide
    The uncompanioned way.

WHO to the grave child-eyes could teach
    Unknown Love's tremor and his play;
The silences that crown his speech,
    His bitter-sweet and mourning way?

Thro' those dark deeps I saw him rise,
    And stir the spirit's soft control,
And shake the imaged world that lies
    Fair on the mirror of her soul.

How oft thro' woodlands undefiled
    She rode amid the spring-tide's stir!
Fierce creatures at her touch were mild
    And dumb things spake for love of her.

Then all at once her heart would beat,
    And from her gaze the gladness died;
She drew the rein, before her feet
    The sunset vales lay glorified.

Alone and ardent, fair and young,
   O woman smit with woman's pain!
O song thro' all her being sung
   Of Love delaying, Love in vain!

That voiceless passion Love had heard,
   Denied it strangely, strangely gave;
Sighed in a smile and sent my bird
   Bright-plumaged o'er the sundering wave.

As though the soul of all things wild,
   The soul of all things brave and free,
Came in the likeness of a child
   From tossing forests over-sea;

And softly to my bosom stole,
   And o'er my heart in freshness blew,
Until that living loving soul
   Became my life, my love anew.

ARETHUSA.

O GENTLE rushing of the stainless stream,
    Haunt of that maiden's dream!
O beech and sycamore, whose branches made
    Her dear ancestral shade!
I call you praying; for she felt your power
    In many an inward hour;
To many a wild despairing mood ye gave
    Some help to heal or save,
And sang to heavenlier trances, long and long,
    Your world-old undersong.
Now therefore, if ye may, one moment show
    One look of long ago;

Create from waving sprays and tender dew
    Her soft fair form anew;
From deepening azure of these August skies
    Relume her ardent eyes!
Or if there may not from your sunlit aisle
    Be born one flying smile,—
In all your multitudinous music heard
    One whisper of one word,—
Then wrap me, forest, with thy blowing breath
    In sleep, in peace, in death;
Bear me, swift stream, with immemorial stir,
    To love, to God, to her.

AUF FLÜGELN DES GESANGES.

GREAT dragon-flies in blazing blue
Across the shimmering river flew;
A dreamy fount of carol played
Thro' calm and ripple, shine and shade.

And all was joyous, all was fair,
Because the golden girl was there;
Her loving eyes illumed that day
The pine-clad winding waterway.

Until it seemed that charmed erelong
By incantation of her song
The broadening deep would flood and flow
From heights of Himalayan snow:—

Her face, in that enchanted hour,
Among the lotos-flowers a flower,
Her whisper mingling, tale for tale,
With roses in the Orient vale.

Then bloomy palms would wave and shed
Their magic slumber overhead,
And Ganges' everlasting stream
Sigh thro' the hushed and holy dream.

UNSATISFACTORY.

'Have other lovers,—say, my love,—
    Loved thus before to-day?'—
'They may have, yes! they may, my love;
    Not long ago they may.'

'But though they worshipped thee, my love,
    Thy maiden heart was free?'—
'Don't ask too much of me, my love;
    Don't ask too much of me!'

'Yet now 'tis you and I, my love,
    Love's wings no more will fly?'—
'If Love could never die, my love,
    Our love should never die.'

'For shame! and is this so, my love,
 And Love and I must go?'—
'Indeed I do not know, my love;
 My life, I do not know.'

'You will, you must be true, my love,
 Nor look and love anew!'—
'I'll see what I can do, my love;
 I'll see what I can do.'

SATISFACTORY.

I

" Do you remember, darling,
   The mocking words you said,—
And snapt with fairy fingers
   And shook your naughty head?
And have you thought it over yet?
   And will my child be true?
And has she loved me long enough
   To know what she can do?"—

2

"Oh I remember nothing,
   Nor mocking words nor true,—
For I remember nothing
   But you, but you, but you!
Forget the men that wooed me,—
   I hate them,—let them go;—
Forget the song I sang to you
   That day I 'did not know'!

3

"Ah! not like this they wooed me,—
   'Twas gamesome girl and boy;—
Sometimes I half was willing
   And often I was coy:
And this I took for love, dear,—
   So little then I knew!
But now I smile to think I thought
   Of any love but you.

SATISFACTORY.

4

"For *this* is quite a strange thing,
    With *this* I cannot play;
At a single look of yours, dear,
    My spirit melts away;
And body and soul are yours, dear,
    I am you, I am not I,
And if you go I'll follow you,
    And if you change, I'll die."—

5

"I've seen in a king's cabinet
    Full many a carven toy;
And Life the Psyche-butterfly
    And Love the running boy;
And Life the altar odorous
    And Love the kindling flame,
And Life the lion amorous
    Which Love was come to tame.

6

But we from sard and sardonyx
　Must grave us gems anew,
If we would have the legend
　Tell truth for me and you!
For Love has caught the butterfly,
　And Love has lit the fire,
And Love has led invincibly
　His lion with the lyre."

'Oh never kiss me; stand apart;
    My darling, come not near!
Be dear for ever to my heart,
    But be not over-dear!'

And while she spake her cheek was flame,
    Her look was soft and wild;
But when I kissed her, she became
    No stronger than a child.—

Ah, love, what wilt thou then apart?
    Thy home is thus and here,—
For ever dearer to my heart,
    And never over-dear.

HESIONE.

In silence slept the mossy ground,
　Forgetting bird and breeze;
In towering silence slept around
　The Spanish chestnut-trees;
Their trailing blossom, feathery-fair,
Made heavy sweetness in the air.

All night she pondered, long and long,
　Alone with lake and lawn;
She heard a soft untimely song,
　But slept before the dawn:
When eyes no more can wake and weep,
A pensive wisdom comes with sleep.

"O love," she said, "O man of men,
    O passionate and true!
Not once in all the years again
    As once we did we do ;
What need the dreadful end to tell?
We know it and we knew it well."

"O love," she said, "O king of kings,
    My master and my joy,
Are we too young for bitter things
    Who still are girl and boy?
Too young we won, we cherish yet
That dolorous treasure of regret."

Then while so late the heavens delayed
    Their solemn trance to break,
Her sad desiring eyes were stayed
    Beyond the lucid lake ;
She saw the grey-blue mountains stand,
Great guardians of the charmèd land.

Above her brows she wove and wound
    Her gold hellenic hair;
She stood like one whom kings have crowned
    And God has fashioned fair;—
So sweet on wakened eyes will gleam
The flying phantom of a dream.

Or so, inarched in veiling vine,
    The Syran priestess sees
Those amethystine straits enshrine
    The sleeping Cyclades;
For Delos' height is purple still,
The old unshaken holy hill.

"O love," she said, "tho' sin be sin,
    And woe be bitter woe,
Short-lived the hearts they house within,
    And they like those will go;—
The primal Beauty, first and fair,
Is evermore and everywhere.

"And when the faint and fading star
    In early skies is sweet,
In silence thither from afar
    Thy heart and mine shall meet;
Deep seas our winged desire shall know,
And lovely summer, lovely snow.

"And whensoever bards shall sing—
    However saints shall pray—
Whatever sweet and happy thing
    The painter brings to day,—
Their heavenly souls in heaven shall be,
And thou with these, and I with thee.

"And God,"—she said, and hushed a while,
    "And God,"—— but, half begun,
Thro' tears serener than a smile,
    Her song beheld the sun:—
When souls no more can dream and pray,
Celestial hope will dawn with day.

NORA.

I.

O NORA knew it, Nora knows
How Love lies hidden in a rose,
And touches mingle, touches part
The trembling flames of heart and heart.

Thrice happy! to have learnt that day
Her virginal bewitching way,
So airy-soft, so winning-wild,
Between the siren and the child.

O Nature's darling, pure and fair
From light foot to irradiant hair!
O Nora, Nora, bright and sweet
From clear brow to impetuous feet!

So glimmered wood and wave between
The starry presence of Undine,
In that first hour her bosom knew
What human hearts are born unto;—

For half-enchanted, half-afraid,
The nymph became a mortal maid;
A dewy light, a dear surprise,
Illumed her visionary eyes.

Then from their deeps a Spirit came;—
Undine was other and the same;—
For past resisting, past control,
Was very Love her very soul.

II.

Last year, where mixed with many a rose
  The gold laburnums wave,
A crimson rosebud Nora chose,
  A bud my Nora gave.

And when the enchanting month anew
    Revived the summer's boon,
And bright again the roses blew,
    And all was joy and June,

A fair twin-bud for my delight
    She from its cluster parts;—
Here are the petals, red and white,
    Shaped like two sister hearts.

And now because the maid is dear
    And ways between us long,—
Because I cannot call her here
    With sighing or with song,—

Across the ocean, swift and soon,
    This faded petal goes,
To her who is herself as June,
    And lovely, and a rose.

THOUGH words of ice be spoken
  And tears of fire be shed,
It seems Love's heart is broken,
  And yet he is not dead:
Whate'er the wild voice utters
  He breathes a still reply;
A bird he is; he flutters
  And yet can never fly.

Unchecked he came, unbidden;
  Unnamed, unknown, he grew;
He wove, unsought, unchidden,
  His old, old charm anew;
And now, though tears upbraid him,
  He smiles and has his way;
A god he is! we made him,
  And yet we cannot slay.

PHYLLIS.

O PAINTER, match an English bloom,
    And give the head an English air,
Then with great grey-blue stars illume
    That face pathetically fair.

As though some sweet child, dowered at will
    With all the wisdom years could send,
Looked up and, like a baby still,
    Became thine equal and thy friend;

And kept the childly curves, and grew
    To woman's shape in wondrous wise,
And with soft passion filled anew
    The sea-like sapphire of her eyes.

Look on her, painter; is there aught
Of well-beloved that is not here?
Could chance or art be guessed or taught
To make the lovely child more dear?

WHEN summer even softly dies,
    When summer winds are free,
A thousand lamps, a thousand eyes,
    Shall glimmer in the sea :
O look how large, behind, below,
The lucid creatures glance and glow!
They strew with soft and fiery foam
Her streaming way from home to home.

So shines the deep, but high above,
    Beyond the cloudy bars,
The old infinity of love
    Looks silent from the stars :—

When parted friends no more avail
Those sleepless watchers shall not fail,
They learn her looks, they list her sighs,
They love her soft beseeching eyes.

Then in the woman's heart is born
   The child's delight anew,
The Highland glory of the morn,
   The rowans bright with dew;
She hears the flooding stream that falls
By those ancestral castle-walls,
Her father's woods are tossing free
Between her and the southern sea.

Or lovely in a lovely place
   One offers as she stands
Sister to sister sweet embrace
   And hospitable hands;
White-robed as once in happy hours
She stood a rose among the flowers,
And heart to heart would speak and tell
The reason why we loved her well.

So in a dream the nights go by,
   So in a dream the days,
Till, when the good ship knows anigh
   The Asian waterways,
From home to home her love shall set
And hope be stronger than regret,
And rest renew and prayer control
Her sweet unblemishable soul.

The waves subside; she stems at last
   That Hellespontine stream;
Her ocean-dreams are overpast,—
   Or is this too a dream?
For child and husband, fast and fain,
Have clasped her in their arms again:—
Let only mothers murmur this,
How babe and mother clasp and kiss.

A CRY FROM THE STALLS.

BEAUTIFUL darling!
 Light of mine eyes!
Gay as the starling
 Shoots thro' the skies;

Swift as the swallow, and
 Soft as the dove;
Hopeless to follow, and
 Maddening to love!

Ah when she dances! and
 Ah when she sings!
Glamour of glances, and
 Rush as of wings,—

Trill as of coming birds
Heard unaware,—
Poise as of humming-birds
Hanging in air!

Starriest, youthfullest
Flower of a face!
Who shall the truthfullest
Tell thee thy grace?

They comprehend it not,
They cannot know;—
Use it not, spend it not,
Spoil it not so!

While the world calls to thee
I sit apart,
I from the stalls to thee
Fling thee my heart!

Bright eyes to measure it!
   Small hands to hold!
Take it and treasure it!
   Lo, it is gold!

Stage-plays have ending, and
   Love's ever new!
Stage-love's pretending, and
   Now for the true!

Fame's voice be dumb to thee!
   Fame's banner furled!
Come with me, come to the
   End of the world!

THE BALLERINA'S PROGRESS,
OR THE POETRY OF MOTION.

Iri, decus cœli, quis te mihi nubibus actam ? —

I. The School.

WITH mantling cheek, with palpitating breast,
See the sweet novice glide among the rest!
O see her from those timorous shoulders fair
Fling back the tossing torrent of her hair!
See half diaphanous and half displayed
The shy limbs gleam, the magic of the maid!
Nor at first seeing wouldst thou deem it true
Such fairy feet such daring deeds could do,
Or Art inborn the maiden shame dispel

From those sweet eyes, that aspect lovable ;—
Yet little by little, as in her ears begin
The thrill and scream of flute and violin,—
O little by little and in a wondrous way
The hid soul hearkens and the limbs obey ;—
As though the starry nature, quenched and hid
Between things impotent and things forbid,
Found thus an air and thus a passion, thus
Were crowned and culminant and amorous,
And dared the best and did it, and became
Vocal, a flying and irradiant flame.

Thus when the Pythian maid no more can bear
The god intolerable and thundering air,
Nor shifting colour and heaving heart contain
Longer the quenchless prophesying pain,—
The more she strives from out her breast to throw
The indwelling monarch of the lute and bow,
The more, the more will mastering Phœbus tire
Her proud lips frenetic and eyes of fire,
Till last, in Delphic measure, Delphic tone,
Bows the wild head, and speaks, and is his own.

II. THE STAGE.

Then flame on flame the immense proscænium
    glows
With magic counterchange of gold and rose,
Then roar on roar, undying and again,
Crash the great bars of that prodigious strain,—
Fire flashed on fire and sound on thunder hurled
Bear from their midst the Wonder of the World.
Lightly she comes, as though no weight she
    ware,
The very daughter and delight of air,—
Lightly she comes, preluding, lightly starts
The breathless rapture to a thousand hearts,
The high flutes hush to meet her, and the drum
Thro' all his deep self trembles till she come:—
Then with a rush, as though the notes had known
After long hope their empress and their own,
She and the music bound, and high and free
Thro' light and air the music leaps and she:—

So bright, so coruscating, Iris so
Slides the long arch of her effulgent bow;
Rose in her wake and azure on her way
A thousand tints bedew the Olympian day;—
She touches earth, and all those hues are one,
And her unbent bow springs into the sun.

I saw, I saw the lovely child,
   I watched her by the way,
I learnt her gestures sweet and wild,
   Her loving eyes and gay.

Her name?—I heard not, nay, nor care,—
   Enough it was for me
To find her innocently fair
   And delicately free.

Oh cease and go ere dreams be done,
   Nor trace the angel's birth,
Nor find the Paradisal one
   A blossom of the earth!

Thus is it with our subtlest joys,—
How quick the soul's alarm!
How lightly deed or word destroys
That evanescent charm!

It comes unbidden, comes unbought,
Unfettered flees away,—
His swiftest and his sweetest thought
Can never poet say.

M.

CYDIPPE.

All-golden is her virgin head,
   Her cheek a bloomy rose,
Carnation-bright the fluttering red
   That o'er it softly flows,
But neither gem nor floweret vies
With that clear wonder of her eyes.

But twice hath hue like theirs been given
   To be beheld of me,
And once 'twas in the twilight heaven,
   Once in the summer sea;
A yearning gladness thence was born,
A dream delightful and forlorn.

For once in heaven a single star
  Lay in a light unknown,—
A tender tint, more lucid far
  Than all that eve had shown,—
It seemed between the gold and grey
The far dawn of a faery day.

And once where ocean's depth divine
  O'er silvern sands was hung,
Gleamed in the half-lit hyaline
  The hope no song has sung,—
The memory of a world more fair
Than all our blazing wealth of air.

For dear though earthly days may flow,
  Our dream is dearer yet;—
How little is the life we know
  To life that we forget!—
Till in a maiden's eyes we see
What once hath been, what still shall be.

LOVER'S SONG.

I THANK thee, dear, for words that fleet,
   For looks that long endure,
For all caresses simply sweet
   And passionately pure;

For blushes mutely understood,
   For silence and for sighs,
For all the yearning womanhood
   Of grey love-laden eyes.

Oh how in words to tell the rest?
   My bird, my child, my dove!
Behold I render best for best,
   I bring thee love for love.

Oh give to God the love again
Which had from him its birth,—
Oh bless him, for he sent the twain
Together on the earth.

ANTE DIEM.

'O SEEK not with untimely art
  To ope the bud before it blows,
Bewitching from the folded heart
  Reluctant petals of the rose!

Too quickly cherished, quickly dear,
  She came, the graceful child and gay,—
O leave her in her early year
  Till April crimson into May!

The golden sun shall glance and go,
  Shall rest and tremble in her hair;
Beside her cheek shall love to blow
  The soft and kindly English air;—

O leave her glad with such caress,
   In such embraces clasped and free,
Nor teach thy hasty heart to guess
   The woman and the love to be.'

Thus with myself my thoughts complain,
   And so by night shall I be wise,
Till on my heart arise again
   Her open and illumined eyes.

A moment then the past prevails
   And in the man is manhood strong,
Then from the bruisèd soul exhales
   The sweet and quivering flame of song.

Oh if indeed with time and tide
   Too fast the changeful seasons flow,
And loving life from life divide
   And shape and sunder as they go,—

Yet with what airy bonds I may
　Her flying soul shall I retain,
And sometimes, dreaming in the day,
　Shall see her, as she smiled, again:—

A girlish joy shall haunt the spot,
　A presence shall illume the shade,
And unembraced and unforgot
　Shall rise the vision of a maid.

WHY should I strive to express it?
　What should I care?
Ye will not know nor confess it
　How she was fair.
Fades the song ere I begin it,
　Falters and dies:—
Ah! had you seen her a minute,—
　Looked in her eyes!

When she and I shall be lying
　Dust at your feet,
Hours such as these shall be flying,
　Life be as sweet,—
Women as lovely hereafter,
　Tender and wise,
Born with her bloom and her laughter,—
　Not with her eyes!

PREEXISTENCE.

ONCE, and beyond recollection,
    Once, ere the skies were unfurled,
These an immortal affection
    Found at the birth of the world.
Earth was not yet, nor the golden
    Vault of the dawn and the dew;
These in a home unbeholden
    Loved and were true.

Heard ye how each from the other
    Drank interchangeable life?
Call ye them sister or brother,
    Husband, or lover, or wife?
Names of an earthly affection
    Are not so close or so dear;
Spirits beyond recollection
    Loved, and are here.

A SONG.

The pouring music, soft and strong,
    Some God within her soul has lit,
Her face is rosy with the song
    And her grey eyes are sweet with it.

A woman so with singing fired,
    Has earth a lovelier sight than this?
Oh he that looked had soon desired
    Those lips to fasten with a kiss.

But let not him that race begin
    Who seeks not toward its utmost goal;
Give me an hour for drinking in
    Her fragrant and her early soul.

To happier hearts I leave the rest,
    Who less and more than I shall know,
For me, world-weary, it is best
    To listen for an hour and go:

To lift her hand, and press, and part,
    And think upon her long and long,
And bear for ever in my heart
    The tender traces of a song.

HONOUR.

A MAN and woman together, a man and woman apart,
In the stress of the soul's worst weather, the anchorless ebb of the heart,
They can say to each other no longer, as lovers were wont to say,
'Death is strong, but Love is stronger; there is night and then there is day';
Their souls can whisper no more, 'There is better than sleep in the sod,
We await the ineffable shore, and between us two there is God':

Nay now without hope or dream must true friend
sever from friend,
With the long years worse than they seem, and
nothingness black at the end:
And the darkness of death is upon her, the light
of his eyes is dim,
But Honour has spoken, Honour, enough for her
and for him.

Oh what shall he do with the vision, when deep
in the night it comes,
With soul and body's division, with tremor of
dreamland drums;
When his heart is broken and tender, and his
whole soul rises and cries
For the soft waist swaying and slender, the child-
like passionate eyes?
Or where shall she turn to deliver her life from
the longing unrest,
When sweet sleep flies with a shiver, and her
heart is alone in her breast?

It is hard, it is cruel upon her, her soft eyes
　　glow and are dim,
But Honour has spoken, Honour, enough for her
　　and for him.

I had guessed not, did I not know, that the spirit
　　of man was so strong
To prefer irredeemable woe to the slightest sha-
　　dow of wrong ;
I had guessed not, had I not known, that twain
　　in their last emprize,
Full-souled, and awake, and alone, with the whole
　　world's love in their eyes,
With no faith in God to appal them, no fear of
　　man in their breast,
With nothing but Honour to call them, could yet
　　find Honour the best,—
Could stay the stream of the river and turn the
　　tides of the sea,
Give back that gift to the giver, thine heart to
　　the bosom of thee.

ELODIA.

O SUDDEN heaven! superb surprise!
  O day to dream again!
O Spanish eyebrows, Spanish eyes,
  Voice and allures of Spain!

No answering glance her glances seek,
  Her smile no suitor knows;
That lucid pallor of her cheek
  Is lovelier than the rose;—

But when she wakens, when she stirs,
  And life and love begin,
How blaze those amorous eyes of hers,
  And what a god within!

I watched her heart's arising strife,
  Half eager, half afraid;
I paused; I would not wake to life
  The tinted marble maid.

But starlike through my dreams shall go,
  Pale, with a fiery train,
The Spanish glory, Spanish glow,
  The passion which is Spain.

GABRIELLE.

O SCARLET berries sunny-bright!
   O lake alone and fair!
O castle roaring in the night
   With blown Bohemian air!
O spirit-haunted forest, tell
The hidden heart of Gabrielle!

Ah, the superb and virgin face!
   Ah once again to see
Transparent thro' the Austrian grace
   The English purity!
To hear the English speech that fell
So soft and sweet from Gabrielle!

So best, but if it be not so
  Yet am I well content
To think that all things yonder grow
  Stately and innocent;
To dream of woods that whisper well,
And light, and peace, and Gabrielle.

ÉCHOS DU TEMPS PASSÉ.

I

'OH hush,' I cried, 'that thrilling voice,
   That shepherd's plaint no more prolong,
Nor bid those happy loves rejoice
   Thro' feigned rusticities of song!
Too soft a passion through thee sings,
   Too yearning-sweet the phrases flow;
Too deep that music strikes, and brings
   The tears of long ago.

2

'Ah! let me keep my frozen peace,
　　Forget with years the ardent boy,
And face the waking world, and cease
　　To dream of passion, dream of joy!
And yet this heart how strangely yearned!
　　How seemed the dream more true than day!
What flame was that which through me burned,
　　And burns, and fades away?'

3

But she, whose young blood softly stirred
　　Had bid the unconscious maiden sing,
Heart-whole, and simply as a bird
　　That feels the onset of the spring,—
She from mine eyes their secret drew,
　　Learnt from my lips the lover's tone,
And in my soul's confusion knew
　　The impulse of her own.

4

Who is herself my vision's truth,
    Herself my heart's unknown desire,
Herself the hope that led my youth
    With counterchange of cloud and fire;—
Then let her sing as Love has willed
    Of mimic loves that die in air,—
A deeper strain my soul has filled,
    Herself the music there.

THE RENEWAL OF YOUTH.

ARGUMENT.

THE poem opens with a recurrence to previous expressions of unrest and baffled inquiry into the problems of the unseen world (1—22). It is intimated that the present reflections are made from a point of view which gives their author a subjective satisfaction, though he expressly disclaims the power of conducting other minds to the same point (23—32). Since, however, many persons have attained, by various pathways, to some form of faith or peace, it is thought that they may be interested in a sketch of some of the feelings to which an assured hope of immortality gives rise (33—56). One of the simplest of such feelings is the impulse of enterprise and curiosity evoked by the hope of being ultimately able to explore the mysteries of the starry heavens (57—80). Yet it is plain that such investigations,—which may be carried to an inconceivable point even by men still living on our planet,—can afford no real insight into a spiritual world (81—92). The universe, as spiritually conceived, can be apprehended only by the development and elevation of the soul herself (93—106). Such spiritual apprehension may indeed be plausibly derided as imaginary, and compared to the search for San Borondon,—the Aprositus or 'Unapproachable Island' of Ptolemy, —which under certain atmospheric conditions is still apparently visible from the Peak of Teneriffe, but which consists in reality of a bank of vapour (107—126). In reply to this, the difficulty of advancing adequate credentials for any announcement of spiritual discovery is fully admitted, but the analogy of the quest of San Borondon is met with the case of Columbus, who, starting himself also from the Canaries on an adventure in which few sympathized, discovered a real country (127—142). Men, however, who suppose themselves to discern spiritual verities must fully acquiesce in being considered dreamers (143—158). They do not look, in fact, for popular applause, but draw a peculiar delight from the interpenetration of the common scenes of life by their far-reaching memories, meditations, and hopes (159—202). Among these meditations the question of repeated existence on this planet, whether before or after our present life, naturally occurs (203—214). However this may be, death must be regarded as a deliverance, and life on earth as a tumult of sensations through which the main current of our spiritual being should run untroubled and strong, like a river through a clamorous city, or like Aeneas marching through the phantoms of the under-world (215—252). No exemption, indeed, can be promised from sorrow; but under the influence of these great hopes sorrow will be divested of its former bitterness, and felt to be directly educative (253—280). Nor, assuredly, could any conception of a future life be satisfactory which did not involve perpetual effort and consequent advance, — an advance whose ultimate goal seems to lie largely in an increased power of spiritually helping other souls (281—296). It need not be presumptuous to aspire to such developments, however remote from man's present insignificance, since the longest periods which astronomy can measure need bring no cessation to the upward efforts of the soul (297—308). In view of such high possibilities, a stern and thorough spiritual training is to be desired (309—318). A frequent experience shows that the stimulating influence of sorrows endured in common, or even of the separation of death, is usually needed to raise human love to the highest development of which earth admits (319—336). In like manner, all surrounding circumstances, of whatever kind, should be used as means of self-improvement. If they be uncongenial, they may be made to give stoical strength

(337—344). And, on the other hand, artistic and emotional enjoyment, instead of alluring the soul earthwards, may stimulate her progress by suggesting the loftier delights to which she may in time rise (345—360). Art, indeed, in all its manifestations, seems directly to suggest an ideal world (361—364). This is true of Poetry (365—378), and of Painting,—as Tintoret's 'Paradise' may serve to indicate (379—400). With Music this is markedly the case; for although, as in operas of Mozart's, Music gives full voice to human love, she also (especially in the hands of Beethoven) creates the impression that she is perpetually overpassing the range of definable, or even of mundane, emotion (401—418). Nor does this impression seem referable to any purely subjective element in composer or auditor (419—430). It may rather be conceived as the necessary result of the position of Music as a representative of the laws and emotions of a supersensual world (431—446). Such Love, moreover, as can be experienced on earth is felt at its highest moments to be only an earnest of what may exist elsewhere (447—458). Nay, even if already felt as complete and satisfying, it must not limit its outlook to this life alone (459—470). Yet, on the other hand, the love felt on earth is truly sacred and permanent, and, as we may believe, will never be forgotten by the soul at any stage of advance (471—498). Finally, it is by maintaining life and love at a high degree of energy that we may hope to penetrate ever nearer to the central and divine life (499—518). And in the profound peace which even on earth may accompany this sense of progressive union with the divine, all personal fear and sorrow,— nay even the anguish of desolating bereavement,—may disappear in a childlike faith (519—548).

THE RENEWAL OF YOUTH.

'Ah, could the soul, from all earth's loves set free,
Plunge once for all and sink them in the sea!
Then naked thence, re-risen and reborn,
Shine in the gold of some tempestuous morn,
With one at last to lead her, one to say—
Come hither, hither is thy warlike way!—
Oh that air's deep were thronged from heaven to hell
With shadowy shapes of barque and caravel,
On rays of sunset and on storms that roll
Swept to a last Trafalgar of the soul!'   10

Ah me! how oft have such wild words confessed
The impetuous urgence of a fierce unrest,

When all the embracing earth, the inarching blue,
Seemed the soul's cage no wings might battle
    through,
And Faith was dumb, or all her voices vain,
Against the incumbent night, the baffling pain ;—
Dumb, till some mastering call, with broadened
    scope,
Should ring the evangel of authentic hope,—
Show the strong soul, aroused, alive, afar,
From death's pale peace delivered into war,— 20
Bid Life live on, nor Love disdain to sing
Mid fading boughs his anthems of the spring.

Nathless, my soul, if thou perchance hast heard,
I say not whence, some clear disposing word,—
If on thy gaze has oped, I say not where,
Brighter than day the light that was thy prayer,—
Thereon keep silence; who of men will heed
That secret which to thee is life indeed ?
For if thou sing of woes and wandering, then
Plain tale is thine, and words well-known to men ; 30

But if of hope and peace, then each alone
Must find that peace by pathways of his own.

Yet many are there who some glimpse have seen
From this world's cave of waters wide and green,
Who have striven as strive they might, and found
    their rest
Each in such faith as for each soul is best;—
To such thy message lies, nor needs inquire
What path has led them there where they desire;—
If in sweet trance it hath to some been given
To stand unharmed in the outmost porch of
    heaven,—   40
To have seen the flamy spires of mounting prayer,
Crowns of election hanging in the air,
And guardian souls, and whatso waits to bless
Man all unknowing in all his loneliness;—
Or if the Father for their need have sent
No separate call nor strange admonishment,
Only such hopes as in the spirit spring
With a new calm that brooks not questioning,

Such loves as lift the ennobled life away
From earth and baseness thro' their native day, 50
Such faith as shines, far-off and undefiled,
Guessed in the glad eyes of a stainless child.

For such as these find thou, my heart, a voice
With souls rejoicing gravely to rejoice,
For souls at peace obscurely to express
Gleams of the light which cheers their steadfastness.

Ah me, how oft shall morn's pellucid ray
Stir the high heart for the unknown wondrous way!
How oft shall evening's slant and crimson fire
Immix the earthly and divine desire! 60
What yearning falls from twilight's shadowy dome
For the unchanged city and the abiding home!

Yet chiefliest when alone the watcher sees
Thro' the clear void the sparkling Pleiades,
Or marks from the underworld Orion bring
His arms all gold, and night encompassing,—
With night's cold scent upon his soul is borne
Firewise a mystic longing and forlorn

THE RENEWAL OF YOUTH.

To strike one stroke and in a moment know
Those hanging Pleiads, why they cluster so;— 70
Thro' night to God to feel his flight begun,
And see this sun a star, that star a sun.
  How might one watch the inwoven battalions sweep,—
A dance of atoms,—drifting in the deep!
Ah, to what goal—firm-fixed or flying far—
Drives yon unhurrying undelaying star?
Thro' space, if space it be, past count or ken,—
Thro' time, if that be time, not marked of men,—
From what beginning, what fire-fountain hurled
  Burst the bright streams, and every spark a world? 80

And yet, methinks, men still to be might learn
Whatever eye can fathom, sense discern,
Might note the ether's whirl, the atom's play,
The thousand secrets thronging on the ray,—
Till for that knowledge' sake they scarce could bear
Veilless the tingling incidence of air;—

And yet no nigher for all their wisdom grew
To the old world's life, and pulse that beats
        therethro',
While round them still, with every hour that rolls,
Swept some unnoted populace of souls,—   90
Undreamt-of lay, as ere earth's life began,
The open secret and the end of man.

O living Love, that art all lives in one!
Soul of all suns, and of all souls the sun!
Earth, that to chosen eyes canst still display
The untarnished glory of thy primal day;—
Blue deep of Heaven, for purged sight opening
        far
Beyond the extreme abysm and smallest star;—
By subtler sense must those that know thee know;
Thy secret enters with a larger flow;   100
On her own deeps must the soul's gaze begin
And her whole Cosmos lighten from within,—
Showing what once hath been, what aye must be,
Her Cause at once and End, her Source and Sea,—

Felt deeplier still, as still she soars the higher,
Her inmost Being, her unfulfilled Desire.

'Ah dreamers!' some will say, 'whose wildered
  ken
Shapes in the mist a Hope denied to men!
Too happy! hard to find and hard to keep
Such mythic haven in the guideless deep!   110
Ye think ye find; and men there are who thus
Themselves the enchanted isle Aprositus
Have seen from Teneriffe; to them was known
The eastward shadow of its phantasmal cone,
And the blue promontory, and vale that fills
That interspace of visionary hills;—
They saw them plain; yet all the while they wist
That San Borondon is but of the mist,
And such bold sailors as have thither prest
Come bootless back from the unrewarding quest; 120
Or if, they say, they touch it, they are driven
Far forth by all the angered winds of heaven,
And nevermore win thither, nevermore

Tread with firm feet that legendary shore,
Retrack the confluent billows, or survey
From poop or prow the innavigable way.'

Must then all quests be nought, all voyage vain,
All hopes the illusion of the whirling brain?
Or are there eyes beyond earth's veil that see,
Dreamers made strong to dream what is to be? 130
How should such prophet answer that his faith
Were in firm land and not a floating wraith?
What skill should judge him? who to each assign
The secret calling and the sight divine?

Say, by what grace was to Columbus given
To have pierced the unanswering verge of seas
  and heaven,
To have wrung from winds that screamed and
  storms that fled
Their wilder voice than voices of the dead;
Left the dear isles by Zephyr overblown,
Hierro's haven and Teyde's towering cone, 140

And forth, with all airs willing and all ways new,
Sailed, till the blue Peak melted in the blue?

And these too, these whose visionary gaze
Haunts not those weltering crimsoned waterways,
Whose dream is not of summer and shining seas,
Ind, and the East, and lost Atlantides;—
Who are set wholly and of one will to win
Kingdoms the spirit knows but from within,—
Whose eyes discern that glory glimmering through
The old earth and heavens that scarcely veil the
   new;—   150
Let them say plainly; 'Nay, we know not well
What words shall prove the tale we have to
   tell;
Either we cannot or we hardly dare
Breathe forth that vision into earthly air;
And if ye call us dreamers, dreamers then
Be we esteemed amid you waking men;
Hear us or hear not as ye choose; but we
Speak as we can, and are what we must be.'

Nor much, in very sooth, shall these men need
The world's applausive smile or answering meed; 160
Whose impulse was not of themselves, nor came
With Phœbus' call and whispering touch of Fame,
But for no worth of theirs, and past their will,
Fell like the lightning on the naked hill.

To them the aspects of the heavens recall
Those strange and hurrying hours that were their
  all;
For to one heart her bliss came unaware
Under white cloudlets in a morning air;
Another mid the thundering tempest knew
Peace, and a wind that where it listed blew; 170
And oped the heaven of heavens one soul before
In life's mid crash and London's whirling roar;—
Ay, and transfigured in the dream divine
The thronged precinct of Park and Serpentine,
Till horse and rider were as shades that rode
From an unknown to an unknown abode,
And that grey mere, in mist that clung and curled,
Lay like a water of the spirit-world.

Or long will one in a great garden stray
Thro' sunlit hours of visionary day, 180
Till, in himself his spirit deepening far,
The things that are not be the things that are,
And all the scarlet flowers and tossing green
Seem the bright ghosts of what elsewhere hath been,
And the sun's gold phantasmal, ay, and he
A slumbering phantom who has yet to be.

Or one from Plato's page uplifts his head,
Dazed in that mastering parley of the dead,
Till at dark curfew thro' the latticed gloom
What presence feels he in his lonely room, 190
Where mid the writ words of the wise he stands
Like a strange ghost in many-peopled lands,
Or issuing in some columned cloister, sees
Thro' the barred squares the moon-enchanted trees ;
Till, when his slow resounding steps have made
One silence with their echoes and the shade,
How can he tell if for the first time then
He paces thus those haunts of musing men,

Or once already, or often long ago,
In other lives he hath known them and shall
    know,   200
And re-incarnate, unremembering, tread
In the old same footsteps of himself long dead?

Ay, yet maybe must many an age have past
Ere on this old earth thou have looked thy last;
Oft shall again thy child-eyes opening see
A strange scene brought by flashes back to thee;
Full oft youth's fire shall leap thy veins within,
And many a passion stir thee, many a sin,
And many a spirit as yet unborn entwine
Love unimagined with new lives of thine,   210
Ere yet thou pass, with thy last form's last breath,
Through some irremeable gate of death,
And earth, with all her life, with all her lore,
Whirl on, of thee unseen for evermore.

Ah, welcome then that hour which bids thee lie
In anguish of thy last infirmity!

Welcome the toss for ease, the gasp for air,
The visage drawn, and Hippocratic stare;
Welcome the darkening dream, the lost control,
The sleep, the swoon, the arousal of the soul! 220

Stayed on such hope, what hinders thee to live
Meanwhile as they that less receive than give?
Short time thou tarriest; wherefore shouldst thou
    then
Envy, or fear, or vex thyself with men?
Only care thou that strong thy life and free
Inward and onward sweep into the sea;
That mid earth's dizzying pains thou quit thee well,
Whose worst is now, nor waits a darker hell.

So,—round his path their lair tho' Centaurs made,
Harpies, and Gorgons, and a Threefold Shade,—230
Yet strove the Trojan on, nor cared to stay
For shapes phantasmal flown about his way;
But with sword sheathed in scorn, and heart
    possest
With the one following of the one behest,

THE RENEWAL OF YOUTH.

Beheld at last that folk Elysian, where
Their own sun gilds their own profounder air,—
Found the wise Sire, and in the secret vale
Heard and returned an unambiguous tale.
 Or so this ancient stream thro' London flows,
Her tumult round him gathering as he goes; 240
All day he bears the traffic, hears the strife,
Reflects the pageant of that changeful life;
Then day declines; men's hurrying deeds are done;
Falls the deep night, and all their fates are one;
Their hopes, their fears, a truce imperious keep;
Sorrows and joys are stilled at last to sleep;
From dark to dark the dim-lit river rolls,
A silent highway thro' that place of souls;
As if he only of all their myriads knew
What sea unseen all streams are travelling to, 250
And on swirled eddy and silent onset bare
That city's being between a dream and prayer.

 Ay, thou shalt mourn, my friend, yet not as when
Thou hadst fain been blotted from the roll of men,

Fain that what night begat thee and what day bare
Might sweep to nothing in the abyss of air,
And the earth engulf and the ocean overflow
Thy stinging shame, the wildness of thy woe.
For now thine anguish suddenly oft shall cease,
Caught in the flow of thy perpetual peace,   260
Nor aught shall greatly trouble or long dismay
Thy soul forth-faring thro' the inward day,—
Strong in that sight, and fashioned to sustain
Gladly the purging sacrament of pain;—
Ay, to thank God, who in his heightening plan
Hath chosen to show thee the full fate of man;—
Who not in peace alone hath bid thee go,
But thro' gross darkness, and a wildering woe;
With all his storms hath vext thee, and opprest
With wild despair thy lonely and labouring
    breast;   270
Till there hath somewhat grown in thee so strong
That neither force nor fear nor woe nor wrong
Can check that inward onset, or can still
Thy heart's bold hope, thy soaring flame of will;—

Since thou hast guessed that on thy side have striven
A host unknown, and hierarchs of heaven;
With whom shalt *thou*, in lands unseen afar,
Renew thy youth and go again to war;—
Ay, when earth's folk are dust, earth's voices dumb,
From world to world shalt strive and overcome. 280

Say, could aught else content thee? which were best,
After so brief a battle an endless rest,
Or the ancient conflict rather to renew,
By the old deeds strengthened mightier deeds to do,
Till all thou art, nay, all thou hast dreamed to be
Proves thy mere root or embryon germ of thee;—
Wherefrom thy great life passionately springs,
Rocked by strange blasts and stormy tempestings,
Yet still from shock and storm more steadfast grown,
More one with other souls, yet more thine own?—290
Nay thro' those sufferings called and chosen then
A very Demiurge of unborn men,—

A very Saviour, bending half divine
To souls who feel such woes as once were thine;—
For these, perchance, some utmost fear to brave,
Teach with thy truth, and with thy sorrows save.

That hour may come when Earth no more can
    keep
Tireless her year-long voyage thro' the deep;
Nay, when all planets, sucked and swept in one,
Feed their rekindled solitary sun;—   300
Nay when all suns that shine, together hurled,
Crash in one infinite and lifeless world:—
Yet hold thou still, what worlds soe'er may roll,
Naught bear they with them master of the soul;
In all the eternal whirl, the cosmic stir,
All the eternal is akin to her;
She shall endure, and quicken, and live at last,
When all save souls has perished in the past.

And wouldst thou still thy hope's immenseness
    shun?

Shield from the storm thy soul's course scarce
  begun?   310
These shattering blows she shall not curse but
  bless;
How were she straitened with one pang the less!
Ah, try her, Powers! let many a heat distil
Her lucid essence from the insurgent ill;
Oh roughly, strongly work her bold increase!
Leave her not stagnant in a painless peace!
Nor let her, lulled in howso heavenly air,
Fold her brave pinions and forget to dare!

So thrives not Love; nor his great glory is shed
On thornless summers and a rosy bed;   320
Nor oft mid all things fair and full content
Soars he to rapture, blooms to ravishment;—
But even as Beauty is no vain image wrought
By man's mere senses or adventurous thought,
But founts austere maintain her lovesome youth,
And Beauty is the splendid bloom of Truth;—
So Love is Virtue's splendour; flame that starts
From the struck anvil of impassioned hearts;—

Who though sometimes their Paradisal care
Be but to till Life's field and leave it fair,— 330
For some sweet years charged only to prolong
Their lives' decline in new lives clear of wrong;—
Yet oftener these by sterner lessons taught
Shall know the hours when Love is all or naught,
When strong pains borne together and high deeds
    done,—
Ay, sundering Death by severance welds in one.

Thus be all life thy lesson; raised the higher
By whatsoe'er men scorn, or men desire;—
If lives untuned raise round thee a jarring voice,
Grieve thou for these, but for thyself rejoice; 340
Since fed by each strife won, each strenuous hour,
The strong soul grows; her patience ends in power;
And from the lowliest vale as lightly flown
As from a mount she soars and is alone.

Or thou, if all the arts their wealth have blent
To fashion some still home magnificent,
Wherein at eve thine heart is snared and tame
With lily odours and a glancing flame,

While sighs half-heard of women, and dim things
  fair,
Make the dusk magical and charm the air;— 350
If in that languorous calm thine ardours fade
And half-allured thy soul is half-betrayed,—
Yet with one thought shalt thou again be free,
Rapt in pure peace and inward ecstasy,
Since art and gold are but the shine and show
Of that true beauty which thy soul shall know;—
Ay, these things and things better shall she create
Of her own substance, in her glorious state,
When the unseen hope its visible end shall win
And her best house be builded from within. 360

For Art, the more she quickens, still the more
Must stretch her fair hands to the further shore,
Clearlier thro' fading images descry
Her fadeless home, and truth in phantasy.

Say, hast thou so known Art? hast felt her power
Leap in an instant, vanish in an hour?

Marked in her eyes those gleams auroral play
Mixt with this lumour of the worldly day?
Times have there been when all thy joys were
    naught
To the far following of a tameless thought? 370
When even the solid earth's foundations strong
Seemed but the fabric and the food of Song?—
In what world wert thou then? what spirit heard
That mounting cry which died upon a word?
Whence to thy soul that urgent answer came,
Force none of thine, and high hopes crowned with
    flame?
Which from thy lips fell slow, and lost the while
Their mystic radiance, momentary smile.

    Yea, and unseen things round the Painter stand;
More than his eye directs the master-hand; 380
Dimly and bright, with rapture mixt and pain,
A heavenly image burns upon his brain;—
And many guessed it, but to one alone
God's house was open and His household known,—

Because the Lord had shown it him, and set
Such vision in the heart of Tintoret
That to his burning hurrying brush was given
Sphere beyond sphere the infinite of heaven;—
From light to light his leaping spirit flew,
The heaven of heavens was round him as he
    drew;—   390
Till clear-obscure in eddying circles lay
The golden folk, the inhabitants of day:—
Crowd all his walls, thro' all his canvas throng,
Those eyes enraptured in a silent song,
Hands of appeal, and starry brows that tell
A yearning joy, a wish inaudible.

So mounts the soul; so for her, mounting higher,
Is fresh apocalypse a fresh desire;
Vision is mystery, and Truth must still
By riddles teach, and as she fails fulfil.   400

And Music;—hast thou felt that howsoe'er
Her mastering preludes march upon the air,—

With whatso gladness her full stream she flings
Tumultuous thro' the swirl of terrene things,—
Though she awhile, when the airy notes have flown,
Encompass all men's passion in her own,
Till 'ye who know what thing Love is' can see
His wings in the air vibrate enchantingly,—
Yet oftener, strangelier, are her accents set
Toward hopes unfathomed thro' an unknown
  regret;—   410
Ah listen! tremble! for no earthly fate
Knocks in that occult summons at the gate;—
Hark! for that wild appeal, that fierce acclaim
Cry to no earthly love with earthly flame;—
The august concent its joyaunce whirls away
From thy soul's compass thro' the ideal day;—
The lovely uplifted voice of girl or boy
Stirs the full heart with something strange to joy.

 Then hadst thou thought that still the Thracian
  sent
 Thro' all the chords his infinite lament,   420

Because himself, the minstrel sire of song,
Had loved so passionately, mourned so long,
And taught his seven sweet strings a sighing tone,
And made their wail the answer of his own?
   Or must thou deem 'twas but some Past of thine
Confused the stream of Music's cry divine,
Because her entering Orphic touch revealed
Shrines ruined now, bride-chambers shut and
    sealed,
And thrilling through thee a gleam unwonted
    shed
On loves long lost, and days immortal dead? 430
   Not so, but Music is a creature bound,
A voice not ours, the imprisoned soul of sound,—
Who fain would bend down hither and find her
    part
In the strong passion of a hero's heart,
Or one great hour constrains herself to sing
Pastoral peace and waters wandering;—
Then hark how on a chord she is rapt and flown
To that true world thou seest not nor hast known,

Nor speech of thine can her strange thought unfold,
The bars' wild beat, and ripple of running gold, 440
Since needs must she the unending story tell
Of such sweet mates as with her for ever dwell,
Of very Truth, and Beauty sole and fair,
And Wisdom, made the sun of all that air,
Where now thou art not, but shalt be soon, and thus
Scale her high home, and find her glorious.

And Love? thine heart imagined, it may be,
Himself the Immortal here had lodged with thee?
Thou hadst clomb the heaven and caught him in
   the air,
And clasped him close and felt that he was
   fair?— 450
He hath but shown thee, when thou call'dst him
   sweet,
His eyes' first glance, and shimmer of flying feet,—
He hath but spoken, on his ascending way,
One least word of the words he hath yet to say,—

Who in the true world his true home has made
With fair things first-begotten and undecayed,—
Whereof thou too art, whither thou too shalt go,
Live with Love's self, and what Love knows shalt know.

Ah sweet division, excellent debate
Between this flesh and that celestial state, 460
When Love, long-prayed, hath wrought thee now and here
Peace in some heart so innocently dear
That thought of more than what before thee lies
Seems a mere scorn of present Paradise;
While yet Love rests not so, nor bates his breath
To name the stingless names of Eld and Death;
Knowing, through change without thee and within
His force must grow and his great years begin;—
Knowing himself the mightiest, Death the call
To his high realm and house primordial. 470

Ah, may the heart grow ever, yet retain
All she hath once acquired of glorious gain!
May all in freshness in her deeps endure
Which once hath entered in of high and pure,
Nor the sweet Present's dearness wear away
The grace and power of the old God-given day!
  Nay, as some world-wide race count most divine
Of all their temples one first lowly shrine,
Whereat the vow was pledged, the onset sworn,
Which swept their standards deep into the
    Morn,—   480
So, howsoe'er thy soul's fate bear her far
Thro' counterchanging heaven and avatar,
Still shall her gaze that earliest scene survey
Where eyes heroic taught the heavenly way,
Where hearts grew firm to hold the august desire
Though sea with sky, though earth were mixt
    with fire,—
Where o'er themselves they seized the high con-
    trol,
Each at the calling of the comrade soul.

Ay, in God's presence set them, let them see
The lifting veil of the inmost mystery,   490
Even then shall they remember, even so
Shall the old thoughts rise, and the old love's
    fountain flow.

Ah Fate! what home soe'er be mine at last,
Save me some look, some image of the Past!
O'er deep-blue meres be dark cloud-shadows driven;
Veil and unveil a storm-swept sun in heaven;—
Cold gusts of raining summer bring me still
Dreamwise the wet scent of the ferny hill!

Live then and love; thro' life, thro' love is won
All thy fair Future shall have dared and done: 500
Whate'er the æons unimagined keep
Stored for thy trial in the viewless deep;—
Though thy sad path should lead thee unafraid
Lonely thro' age-long avenues of shade;—
Though in strange worlds, on many a ghostly morn,
Thy soul dishomed shall shudder and be forlorn;—

THE RENEWAL OF YOUTH.

Yet with thee still the World-soul's onset goes;
Wind of the Spirit on all those waters blows;
Still in all lives a Presence inlier known
Is Light and Truth and all men's and thine own ; 510
Still o'er thy hid soul brooding as a dove
With Love alone redeems the wounds of Love;
Still mid the wildering war, the eternal strife,
Bears for Life's ills the healing gift of Life.

Live thou and love! so best and only so
Can thy one soul into the One Soul flow,—
Can thy small life to Life's great centre flee,
And thou be nothing, and the Lord in thee.

And therefore whoso reaches, whoso knows
This ardent peace, this passionate repose,— 520
In whomsoe'er from the heart forth shall swell
The indwelling tide, the inborn Emmanuel,—
Their peace no kings, no warring worlds destroy,
No strangers intermeddle and mar their joy;
These lives can neither Alp on Alp upborne
Hurl from the Glooming or the Thundering Horn,

Nor Nile, uprisen with all his waters, stay
Their march aerial and irradiant way;—
Who are in God's hand, and round about them
    thrown
The light invisible of a land unknown;   530
Who are in God's hand; in quietness can wait
Age, pain, and death, and all that men call Fate:—
What matter if thou hold thy loved ones prest
Still with close arms upon thy yearning breast,
Or with purged eyes behold them hand in hand
Come in a vision from that lovely land,—
Or only with great heart and spirit sure
Deserve them and await them and endure;
Knowing well, no shocks that fall, no years that
    flee,
Can sunder God from these, or God from thee; 540
Nowise so far thy love from theirs can roam
As past the mansions of His endless home.

Hereat, my soul, go softly; not for long
Runs thy still hour from prime till evensong;

Come shine or storm, rejoice thee or endure,
Set is thy course and all thy haven is sure;
Nor guide be thine thro' halcyon seas or wild
Save the child's heart and trust as of the child.

www.ingramcontent.com/pod-product-compliance
Lightning Source LLC
Chambersburg PA
CBHW022007220426
43663CB00007B/1001